HINDU SOCIETY AT CROSS ROADS

HINDU SOCIETY AT CROSS ROADS

by

K. M. PANIKKAR

GYAN

Published by

Gyan Publishing House
5, Ansari Road
Daryaganj, New Delhi-110002
Phone: 011-47034999, 9811692060
E-mail: books@gyanbooks.com

Distribution Network
gyanbooks.com
India, USA, Canada, UK, Australia

ISBN: 978-81-212-8428-8 (HB)
First Published, 1961

2nd Impression 2024

Printed at: Gyan Press, Delhi.

HINDU SOCIETY AT CROSS ROADS
Author: K. M. PANIKKAR

HINDU SOCIETY AT CROSS ROADS

Hindu Society at Cross Roads

by

K. M. PANIKKAR

ASIA PUBLISHING HOUSE
BOMBAY · CALCUTTA · NEW DELHI · MADRAS
LONDON . NEW YORK

Contents

	Page
Introduction	9
The Argument	24
Hindu Social Institutions	29
Untouchability	51
Women in the Hindu Family	57
Custom as King	68
Legislation and Society	78
The Impacts	95
The Prospects	115
Religion and Society	122
Conclusion	130

Art. 15 (I) The State shall not discriminate against any citizen on grounds only of religion, race, caste, sex, place of birth or any of them.

Art. 17 "Untouchability" is abolished and its practice in any form is forbidden. The enforcement of any disability arising out of "Untouchability" shall be an offence punishable in accordance with law.

Art. 38 The State shall strive to promote the welfare of the people by securing and protecting as effectively as it may a social order in which justice, social, economic and political, shall inform all the institutions of the national life.

—The Constitution of India

Introduction

The Hindu society is no longer at cross roads. Since the publication of this book in 1955 the Hindu people have made their choice and have elected to march along the road of progress. When the book was written legislative measures for changing the social structure of Hinduism were under the consideration of Parliament. Bills meant to provide Hindu society with uniform laws in such important matters as marriage and succession were under consideration. The Great Debate was on, but the decision, though never in doubt, had not been finally taken. Today these changes which, it may well be said revolutionise Hindu society, have been placed on the statute book without creating any social or political upheaval.

The Hindu people constitute one of the oldest integrated societies of the world. For over two thousand five hundred years the Hindus have been a people. They had, broadly speaking, an organised social system the main characteristics of which were the same from the Himalayas to Cape Comorin. No doubt the Dharma Sastras and the Grihya Sutras which embody these principles applied only to certain dominant classes and beneath them were many communities professing a wide variety of custom and practice. And yet it is one of the miracles of history that loosely knit though it was, Hindu society has survived over two millenia and half and remains today an active and vigorous society ready to take its place in the world.

Its activity and vigour and its readiness to march with the rest are the outcome of a hundred years of social upsurge and the last twelve years of politicial activity. The Hindu society which the 19th century inherited was very much alive as many reform movements showed, but its social organisation as a whole was moribund. The reasons for the creeping paralysis which seemed to affect the general body of Hindu society I have analysed in the book. The failure to readjust itself by timely and appropriate changes was due to the political circumstances of Indian life. For the first time, after the period of its early integration, Hindu society became armed with the appropriate machinery for effecting change only after the achievement of independence in 1947.

During the last thirteen years of India's independence the new State has undertaken comprehensive legislation affecting many basic aspects of Hindu society. The purpose of the present Introduction is to consider the effect of this complex of legislation.

The most spectacular of the changes which independent India brought about was the abolition of untouchability. That change was brought about by a constitutional provision and from that point of view it is dealt with in the book. But even more significant than the provision in the constitution was the enactment of the Untouchability Offences Act which came into force all over India on the 1st June 1955. Under this Act all Hindu religious institutions have been thrown open to those who were formerly considered as untouchables and consequently were not entitled to worship with caste Hindus. As a result of this legislation the untouchable may use the waters of any stream, tank or well to the extent used by others. Obstruction of access to shores, public restaurants, hotels, places of entertainment and similar facilities is also an offence when it is directed against members of these classes.

Not only has the denial of these rights now been declared an offence, but the law now further provides that when such denial is attempted in the case of one previously classed as untouchable the law would presume that the commission of the forbidden act was on the ground of untouchability.

It would be too much to expect that the practice of untouchability has been totally eradicated from every part of India. It is, however, obvious that not only is it not a part of Hindu social theory but that both the state and the community are actively engaged in removing its effects by a comprehensive programme which includes educational, political and economic action. The importance of adult franchise in awakening the political consciousness of the untouchables need not be emphasised. Politically they have become a major factor and are represented in central and state cabinets. Reserved seats in legislatures, corporations, municipal councils and all other elected bodies, special provisions for recruitment to services, participation in political power, facilities for admission to scientific and technological institutions—these are some of the means used by the Government of India to bring the former untouchables to the level of other communities.

Two other important changes the effects of which are equally far reaching and revolutionary relate to the marriage and succession laws which the Indian Parliament enforced in 1956. Hindu law in respect of these two matters before the present legislation had been determined by ancient texts, modified by local and family customs. Even this was only partially true. Many communities professing the Hindu religion and broadly classified as Hindus were governed by customs which went against the postulates of Hindu law. The significant fact about the new marriage law is that it radically changes the nature of Hindu social structure in three different ways. First from the legal point of view marriage becomes purely contractual, thereby allowing for the first time the right of divorce to Hindu women. While it was true that there were many populous communities where the right of divorce was freely practised it was part of orthodox theory that marriage was a sacramental bond which could be dissolved only by death. So far as women were concerned, orthodox Hindu theory enforced widowhood for life, though again there were many communities within the fold of Hinduism which allowed the marriage of widows.

Secondly the limitations in respect of caste, so far as they applied to marriages, were totally removed. The principle of the Hindu law subject to the exception mentioned later, was that marriages were permitted only within the same caste. The exception is the marriage of a man belonging to a higher caste to a woman of a lower caste, which though not encouraged was considered legal. The very possibility of a lower caste man marrying a higher caste woman was ruled out. It was something too horrible to contemplate. Such a relationship was altogether void and illegal. It may be mentioned that this is practically the only instance where under the British rule the idea of higher and lower castes received official recognition. Under the new law marriage between Hindus of all castes has been made legal. An untouchable man can under the present law marry a Brahmin girl without resorting to the fiction--necessary before—that they did not belong to any religion. This provision is particularly important. The strength of the system of exclusive castes lay in the prohibition of inter-marriage. By permitting marriage between different castes without reference to their superiority or inferiority the new law has struck at the root of caste itself.

The new succession law is another piece of revolutionary legislation which has much greater significance than mere regulation of succession to property. Among the Hindus in the past, as I have emphasised in the text of the book, women, though they suffered from no special social disability, were economically dependent on men. A daughter had no share in her father's property. She was not, as a wife, supposed in orthodox theory to have separate property of her own. The widow's estate was a limited one. In fact the economic condition of Hindu womanhood was in everyway far behind that of others like Muslims and Christians in India. The Succession Act changes all that. It places sons and daughters on an equal footing. The wife and the widow are equally entitled to separate property. It is obvious that in a society where the economic position of woman had become one of total dependence on men this is a far reaching change with great social consequences.

To realise the change that has taken place in the position of women in India it must also be remembered that the constitution provides for the equality of women and men in political matters and throws open to them all avenues of official appointment. This political equality combined with the rights acquired under the marriage and succession Acts gives Hindu women a place in the vanguard of progressive womanhood.

We may also examine briefly how recent legislation has affected the system of caste, the most characteristic institution of Hindu society; one which had been so recognised for long by western observers. It is true that in the legislative activity of the last 12 years there is no measure which directly attacks caste or seeks to abolish it. In fact caste does not lend itself to such direct frontal attack. It is too elusive for direct legislation. And yet it can be said that the legislation of the last few years has more effectively undermined it than all other activity in the past. In the past, as has been argued in the book, the activities of reformers like Ram Mohan Roy and Dayanand Saraswati had only led to the formation of new sects denying caste while the vast body of Hindus remained unaffected. The new legislation does something else. The strength of the caste system lay clearly in the rules relating to marriage. Inter-caste marriages leading to mixture of castes or *Varna Sankara* was considered the greatest of all social evils. It was the nightmare of the Hindu legislators of the past. As we have already seen the present law permits marriage between different castes of Hindus and thus strikes at the root of caste organisation. Unlike local and sectarian movements of the past the attack on caste today is on a general basis, tending not so much to create new sects as in the past as to weaken the system as a whole.

The loosening of caste rigidity has also been greatly assisted by the democratic structure of India's government. In an earlier book on Caste and Democracy (Hogarth Press) the present writer had argued that caste and democracy were based on contradictory assumptions and could not co-exist in the same society. Adult franchise is a great equaliser and this is exactly what has taken place in India. The traditionally higher castes, Brahmins, Rajputs, Khatris, Kayasthas, etc. are numerically smaller in number than those whom they had long been accustomed to consider as lower castes. In the past power and prestige had been on the basis of caste and landed property. Land legislation had already pulled down one of the two props of this social organisation. Election based on adult franchise pulled down the other.

The one result of the enforcement of adult franchise has been that the so-called lower classes have everywhere realised their strength and begun to assert themselves politically. In every province this has been the marked feature of Indian political life during the last two general elections. Thus in Madras, for example, which had, in the past, been the citadel of Brahmin orthodoxy, political authority has as a result of elections based on adult franchise passed into the hands of others. Similar has been the case in Rajasthan where the Rajputs, after centuries of political dominance, have today become an insignificant minority without effective authority in politics or prestige in social life.

Though the facts stated above could not be contested one often hears the cry that caste, far from dying down, is a growing influence in politics; that "casteism" is a new factor of importance which is mis-shaping Indian democracy. The allegation it must be noticed comes from the higher castes who find their position untenable in the face of the rising influence of those whom till recently they had considered as belonging to the lower orders. Undoubtedly the lower castes everywhere have in a measure made a concerted effort to get rid of the age long authority of the higher castes in Hindu social and political life. That is one of the most welcome signs of the effective functioning of democracy in India.

The cumulative effect of all this, the social legislation as it affects the Hindus, the working of democratic institutions and the planned process of industrialisation has been to effect a major transformation among the Hindu people. It has in effect become a single community living under a unified system of laws relating to marriage, succession, adoption, etc. From an inchoate mass of units it is now well on the way of becoming a single integrated community. Today the Hindu whether he comes from Cape Comorin or Himachal Pradesh, from Orissa or Rajasthan, lives under a single modern and rational system of laws. The customs and practices which had reduced

Hinduism to a living museum of anthropology have been swept away and today the Hindus can claim that they represent not merely a civilisation, an outlook on life, but are a single people.

The difference between the earlier integration which gave birth to the Hindu people and the social revolution which has taken place is that what was achieved in the past was the creation of a dominant society which spread all over India and gave to the Hindus a unity at the top. For that period it was a great achievement. But beneath the top layer was the vast body of unrelated social units grouped together as castes who followed their own laws and customs without reference to Hindu social philosophy. Besides, there were also the millions of untouchables and other backward classes who were separated by a deep and unbridgeable gulf from the social life of Hinduism. The great Poona fast of Mahatma Gandhi was an affirmation of the single fact that, though socially separate, the untouchables were Hindus by religion and any attempt to make it impossible to integrate them into Hindu society would be resisted by the Hindus by every means at their disposal. The integration that is taking place now is thus a consummation and fulfilment of the great work which was begun in the centuries before Buddha and continued till the time of the Guptas.

The continued existence of Hindu society long after political power had disappeared from the Hindus and the machinery of reorganisation was denied to them is as I have said one of the miracles of history. In spite of every kind of internal and external pressure it continued to maintain its separate entity. It kept in tact its institutions and its social structure. Over a long period, it had become immobile, fragmented and to a degree impervious to progressive ideas. Yet it was alive. Every generation showed signs of life, but such life led only to further fragmentation by the creation of new sects. Every new impact produced new sects.

At the beginning of the 19th century, over large areas, Hindu society seemed to be on the verge of dissolution. The missionaries at Serampore and later even Thomas Babington Macaulay thought so. But the impact with the West revived the spirit of the Hindu society, a fact which must have come as a surprise to its critics in the West. The Hindu reformation of the 19th century is one of the major developments of the period, the significance of which historians have not yet recognised. It is that reformation which not only laid the basis for India's independence but enabled her to effect a transformation of Hindu society by a rapid and peaceful process of legislation.

The mind of India had been converted to these changes even under the British period. The abolition of untouchability was a plank in Mahatma Gandhi's programme from 1919. Equal status for women was a demand which had been raised for many decades. The change of marriage law, women's right to property and other reforms were among the accepted items of liberal political thinking. A century and a half of contact with the West and education in western institutions and more than a quarter of a century of mass agitation enabled the ideas of reform to gain ascendancy over the public mind. All that remained to be done was to utilise the dynamism of the revolution to give shape and form to the ideas already accepted. Thus this transformation is basically a fulfilment. No doubt it involved the discarding of many customs and practices which had been associated with the Hindu people. But it also involved the broadening of the basis of Hindu life incorporating within its society millions who had been kept out and held down by harsh social practices. As a result of these changes the Hindu people today stand forth as a society moved by progressive ideas, based on equality, where women have the same rights as men, where men are no longer held down by ties of caste, where social relationship is not being continuously fragmented. No longer at Cross Roads the Hindu society has again started on its march of progress.

New Delhi Dussehra 1960.

The Argument

With the independence of India, Hindu society faces a new situation which constitutes a challenge to her age-old institutions. During the period of British authority over India, the pressure of new forces was originally directed against the Hindu religion in the mistaken belief that it was the religion of the Hindus and not their social organisation that stood in the way of progress. Foreign critics identified the Hindu religion with the social customs prevalent in India and went on to argue from that identification that conversion to other socio-religious organisations alone provided the way for progress. Among the more enlightened Hindus themselves, at one time this view gained wide acceptance. Most of the reform movement of the last century were, it will be remembered, directed against orthodox Hinduism. They proceeded on the assumption that what was necessary was a purification of the Hindu religion. The Brahmo Samaj, the Arya Samaj and other similar movements, which were started with the laudable object of reforming Hindu society confused the main issue and organised themselves on the basis of a reform of religion. This basic misconception had two very significant results. It aroused the dormant powers of the Hindu religion which called forth from its ancient armoury all its weapons to defend its institutions, right or wrong. Practices which had authority neither in religion nor in tradition, came to be regarded as fundamental. Even the self-immolation of widows, which was never widely prevalent and which certainly had no sanction in religion found its defenders at one time. Secondly, it made even the internal reorganisation of Hindu society difficult as reformers came to be identified with the thought and practice of other religions.

The attack on religion has definitely failed now. Even the most ardent workers in the mission field do not have any longer the hope of converting India to Christianity. Equally decisive has been the failure of movements from inside which aimed at a large-scale reform of religious ideas. Hindu religion has emerged triumphant from the struggle and today does not feel her supremacy challenged from any side. But the problem of the Hindu social organisation has remained materially unchanged except that it has now come to be recognised that its solution does not lie through the machinery of religion. It is the Hindu society that has to be basically reorganised and not the Hindu religion.

The thesis which I shall endeavour to establish in the following pages may briefly be stated as follows:

(i) The social organisation of the Hindus is the result of unregulated growth which through historical reasons came to be stunted in its early stages;

(ii) The fragmentation of social feeling is the outstanding characteristic of the Hindu society and this fragmentation is based on the twin-institutions of joint family and caste;

(iii) The institutions of the Hindu people are unconnected with their religion and are based wholly on law and custom and are therefore secular;

(iv) Being based on law and custom,

> they require continuous re-examination and modification through legislation.

It is further the basic argument of this book that the degeneration of the Hindu people was due to the prolonged absence of legislative authority, following the breakdown of the political power of Hinduism. The co-existence for over 600 years of a dominant society (Islam) organised on the basis of a revealed law also led to the crystallisation of institutions and customs which, *by analogy,* came to be considered as sacred by the groups into which society was divided. On the basis of these arguments it is sought to prove that the regeneration of the Hindu people is possible only by emphasising the secular character of their social institutions, and by giving them the framework of a national law which will slowly transform them from an inchoate mass of unrelated groups into a single Hindu community.

The problem facing the Hindus may therefore be formulated as a rethinking of social values, a reorganisation of institutions and a divorce between law and custom on the one hand and religion on the other. This three-fold problem is closely interconnected because the orthodox section of the Hindus holds that every institution however anachronistic like the joint family, and every custom however unreasonable like the denial of inheritance to daughters has the implicit sanction of religion and should be left well alone by legislatures. Fortunately this claim of orthodoxy was, even during the British period, vigorously challenged by the more progressive section among the Hindus, who, at least since the time of Ram Mohan Roy in the early years of the nineteenth century, have increasingly asserted the right and duty of the state to change social institutions and customs by secular legislation.

The Constitution of India has boldly and unequivocally affirmed the right to legislate in social matters. More, it has incorporated as a fundamental right the most far-reaching reform in Hinduism—the abolition of untouchability. A legislating state armed with the full panoply of power has come into existence proclaiming its right and affirming its duty to set right social injustices by legislative action. This is the crisis facing the Hindu society.

Hindu Social Institutions

For a proper understanding of our problem it is necessary to analyse the social structure of Hinduism. This structure revolves round two fundamental institutions, the caste and the joint family. Everything connected with the Hindu people outside their religion, is related to these two institutions. These in fact are the differentiating characteristics of Hindu life. Now, what is caste? Its pervasive character is recognised by all. Its hold on the Hindu mind has been astonishingly firm from the time the Hindus came to be organised as a people. It has so far resisted successfully all attempts meant to undermine it from within and to destroy it from without. And yet no one has yet been able to define it satisfactorily. Then orthodox Hindu view is that society has been divinely ordained on the basis of the four castes—Brahmanas, Kshatriyas, Vaisyas and Sudras; the authority on which this view rests is the statement in the *Purushasūkta* in the Rig Veda that the Brahmin emerged from the head, the

Kshatriya from the arms, the Vaisya from the waist and Sudras from the feet of God. But whatever the origin, it will be obvious even on a casual examination that this four-fold division *is only ideological* and is not in any manner based on the facts of the social system. It is, as we shall try to show, only a schematic arrangement by theorists, who visualised society as organised on a horizontal basis. It is what Hindu sociologists wanted their society to be — a theory of caste-idealism unrelated to actual practice. That the four-fold division never in fact existed can be historically proved. True, the Brahmins, as a caste, separated themselves from the rest, as a result of the development of ritualism in religion and they can legitimately be described as the only integrated caste in Hindu society. But even among them, though a common feeling of Brahminhood existed and exists, there are today no less than 1,800 main sub-castes and perhaps many thousands more whose gradations cannot be properly traced. When there are so many sub-castes among the Brahmins themselves, each of which claims superiority over the other, the idea of the unity of the Brahmin caste vanishes completely. But the Brahmins *are* a caste—

all other castes recognise them to be so. They have a common body of religious rites and broadly speaking a common attitude towards life. This however cannot be said of the other three castes, whose existence as organised entities within the four-fold division is purely notional.

Taking the Kshatriyas—or the so-called warrior classes alleged to have emerged from the arms of Brahma—first, it is a fact that in historical times there was no such caste as the Kshatriyas. Every known royal family from the time at least of Mahapadma Nanda in the fourth century B.C. belonged to non-Kshatriya castes. The Mauryas were known to be Sudras. The Imperial Guptas claimed to be Vaisyas. The Bharasivas were Brahmins. Where did the Kshatriya community disappear after the time of the Nandas in the fourth century B.C.?

The more recent pretenders to Kshatriyahood, the Rajputs, can only claim it on the basis of their occupation. The Sisodias of Udaipur, Kshatriyas *par excellence* today, are of Brahmin origin. The greatest of them, Maharana Kumbha, describes himself as a *Vipra* in his inscriptions. The Rashtrakutas or the Rahtors are a southern clan, who came on the stage of history first on the Deccan Plateau. Their migration to the north and to Rajput orthodoxy can be clearly traced in 8th and 9th centuries A. D. of the princely houses who assumed Kshatriyahood in the 19th century, and of the castes which advanced their claims to higher social status, it is not necessary to speak when the caste itself had ceased to exist for at least 2,000 years.

The Vaisyas are equally a theoretical generalisation. The communities which follow trade and commerce as their hereditary profession claim Vaisyahood. As an integrated caste it however does not exist. So far as the Sudras are concerned, they have always been a miscellaneous group, the mass of people within the Hindu pale, who did not have the *samskara* of the holy thread.

There are, however, two facts about the Sudras which are of great significance. In the area to the south of the Godavari, large and powerful communities which were imperfectly integrated into the structure of Hinduism were in the caste hierarchy counted as Sudras, but continued to enjoy the highest social prestige. The Reddys of the Andhra country, the Vellalas of Tamil Nad and the Nayars of Malabar, never accepted the four-fold division and while technically described as Sudras by the Brahmins, enjoyed, as communities, social power similar to that claimed by the mythical Kshatriyas of the north. A second point of significance is that the Sudras seem to have produced an unusually large number of royal families even in more recent times. The Palas of Bengal belonged undoubtedly to that caste. The great Maratha royal houses, whatever their position today, could hardly sustain their genealogical pretentions connecting them with Rajput descent.

The fact is that the four-fold caste is merely a theoretical division of society to which tribes, clans and family groups are affiliated. It is a sociological fiction. Though the four-fold division is purely notional, the theory of society based on it still governs Hindu life. Every one of the innumerable sub-castes claims to belong to one of the four. Thus they place themselves theoretically within the fold of the main ideological castes. It is therefore necessary to examine the principles of this division.

The essential principles of *Chāturvarnya* or the four-fold division are:

(i) Unchangeable inequality based on birth;

(ii) The gradation of professions and their inequality;

(iii) Restrictions on marriage outside one's own group.

A man's caste is decided by birth. From one caste to another there is no passage for the *individual,* though the position is now changing a little for small organised communities as we shall show later. If a man is born a Sudra he remains a Sudra all his life. He must marry only a Sudra and according to caste-theory he should only carry on the professions allotted to a Sudra. How the Brahmin theorists justified the establishment of a society, based on irremovable *inequality* under which the vast majority of the population was forced to accept the stigma of inferiority, need not be discussed here. It constitutes the most interesting example of the overwhelming influence of institutions on the mind of man.

It is however necessary to add that while social inequality based on birth and the prohibitions in regard to marriage continued in force until recently, the attempt to confine castes to separate professions seems never to have succeeded. The earliest available literature gives instances of Brahmins carrying on the professions of medicine, arms and administration. In the *Jatakas* Brahmins are mentioned as traders, hunters and trappers. R. P. Masani quotes the caste of a Kshatriya prince, Kusa, mentioned in one of the Jataka tales, who became an apprentice in turn to a potter, a basket maker, a florist and a cook. Conversely, from even the Vedic days there have been innumerable instances of men born in the lowest rank of caste-society taking to professions which in theory were the monopoly of the other castes. This was to some extent inevitable when following Mahapadma Nanda and the Mauryas many of the royal families came from among the *Sudras*. Even today a large number of the ruling families of India belong to the aboriginal castes, though many have assumed Kshatriyahood or at least advanced claims to higher social status. In the South where of course there were no Kshatriyas, the Brahmins went to the extent of allowing Sudra rulers to assume a second-class Kshatriyahood after a symbolic rebirth through a golden cow!

If the four-fold system of caste was no more than a fiction, a platonic myth, then what is it that so dominated Hindu society in the past and made that society different from all others? What has existed and mattered much more than the notional division into four castes and what to some extent constitutes the evil of "Caste-ism" is the system of innumerable "sub-castes" each divided again and again, converting the Hindu people into an inchoate mass of small units. The three thousand *major* units of caste enumerated in earlier census returns constitute a factor of the highest sociological importance. These castes are rigidly exclusive and each claims superiority over the other. Neither inter-marriage nor "inter-dining" is normally permitted between them. They are aliens to each other in social life.

The operation of this system of sub-castes divides the Hindu people into such small units as to render the development of any common social feeling impossible. In fact it is a negation of the idea of society. The passage from the barbarous to the civilised state of existence has been marked everywhere by an extension of the circle of social activity or to use the words of Durkheim by a widening of the symbiotic circle. In primitive society the individual stands related either to the family or to the tribe which is only the family on a totemic basis. The progress of human civilisation is based on the extension of the principle of thought and activity. Though this is the universal rule, in India after the society passed through its early stages of civilisation, the process was soon reversed. The symbiotic circle, i.e. the circle of social relationship and activity, was continuously narrowed by a system of marriage regulations. The collective consciousness of social life which is the creative force of social activity and is therefore responsible for the highest form of social endeavour, tended to vanish as the marriage relations became more and more rigid.

If instead of being divided into sub-castes, the castes had been integrated into the four ideological divisions, this disastrous fragmentation of society would never have happened. The four castes would have been a simplification of the chaos, the evolution of a general system of order out of the confusing and tragic anarchy which the process of division produced. The conception of the four castes involved the ideal of an integrated society. It was an organisation of people on certain understandable lines. The grim tragedy however is that even this extent of organisation was not found possible and the theory of four castes remained no more than an ideal.

All the attempted justification of caste has been of the four-fold division—that is of the ideal caste-society. But even that system has no religious sanction. As a recent author points out:

"The seers of the early vedic period know nothing of caste. Delve as much as one may into the literature of the period, one discovers only classes not castes. The elements which go to form castes were however there so that gradually a gulf was created between one order and another. For a long time however the conception of social segregation and untouchability was repugnant to the genius of the people who sought unity in variety and dissolved variety in unity. Each class was regarded as an integral part of the fabric of society."*

In fact, caste as a social crystallisation is in-

* "Caste and the Structure of Society" by R. P. Masani—*Legacy of India*, p. 132.

variably a late development in a decaying civilisation. Spengler in his *Decline of the West* analyses the phenomenon as follows: "The distinction between Estate and Caste is that between earliest culture and latest civilisation. In the rise of the prime Estates—noble and priest—the culture is unfolding itself, while the castes are the expression of its definite fellah-state. The Estate is the most living of all culture launched on the path of fulfilment, 'the form that living must itself unfold'. The caste is absolute finishedness, the phase in which development has been succeeded by immutable fixation."*

For long it was the accepted belief among certain sections of Hindus that *Chāturvarnya* was divinely ordained and that *Varna Sankara* or the mixture of castes was the greatest of social evils. But apart from the *Purushasūkta* mentioned above which gives a fanciful and allegorical explanation of the four functions, the existence of a rigid caste society, where profession goes by hereditary descent and marriage between castes is prohibited is not evidenced by the Vedas or by the canonical

* Spengler: *Decline of the West,* Vol. II, p. 333.

literature that is based on them. In fact, the author of Aitareya Brahmana, one of the most sacred books of Brahmin ritual, was the son of a Brahmin *rishi* by a dasyu wife. While therefore it is obvious that caste is a sociological fact and not a religious institution, it is none the less true that all Hindu Dharma Sastras take caste for granted. All the puranas assume the existence of caste and look upon it as a permanent order of society. But the authority for the divine ordinance of caste is not very convincing. In the Gita it is no doubt stated:

Chāturvarnyam maỳa srstam
Guna karma vibhagasah

and this is often quoted as proving conclusively that caste is a divinely ordained institution. But examined carefully it would be seen that Krishna's words constitute a devastating attack on caste and not its justification. Literally translated the passage means: The four-fold order was created by Me *on the basis of quality and action.* It is the most unequivocal repudiation of the divine origin of caste *based on birth,* the most categorical denial of the Brahmin claim of inherent superiority. No one denies functional differentiations based on quality and action. Even in classless societies, people have to be divided into intellectuals, soldiers, workers and peasants, on the basis of *guna* and *karma*. This is all that the Gita teaches and yet by quoting the first line alone without adding the basis on which Krishna claims to have created it, the very purpose of the text, the categorical repudiation of caste-division based on birth, is perverted and it is made to serve the object of proving to the ignorant that the Gita affirms the sanctity of caste.

If thus religion does not, what gives to the system the appearance of religious sanction? The answer is the Hindu Law. The great Hindu Legal Codes are based on the caste system. Manu especially ordains different kinds of punishment for different castes and holds up *varna sankara* or the mixture of castes as the greatest of evils. But no divine character was at any time claimed for the Dharma Sastras, even by the Brahmins themselves. In fact, historical enquiry into the origin of the Hindu Codes establishes beyond doubt the fact that they grew but slowly and therefore did not receive general acceptance for a considerable time.

Another significant fact about the Dharma Sastras, which needs special emphasis, is that while Manu and the other law-givers divide society into four castes, the social fact of innumerable sub-divisions which rendered the four-fold division purely notional and theoretical did not escape them. They explain it unconvincingly as the result of *varna sankara* or caste mixture and give fanciful names to the groups whose existence they cannot deny. It is therefore clear that from the earliest times, whatever the theoretical position, the social organisation of the Hindus was based on innumerable sub-castes, and not on an integrated four-fold division. No religious sanction has ever been claimed for this system of numerous small groups, each segregated from the other, and living in a world of its own. It is essentially a social growth, the result of the anarchy of Hindu social life. This society of sub-castes is so closely connected with and dependent upon that other characteristic of the Hindus, the joint family, that it is to this institution we must now turn to understand the full significance of its disintegrating influence.

Though in theory unconnected, these two institutions, the caste and the joint family are in practice interlocked to an extent which makes them in effect a common institution. The unit of Hindu society is not the individual but the *joint family.* The widest expression of this family is the "sub-caste" which often consists only of a few joint families which intermarry and "inter-dine" among themselves. Beyond this extended joint family the Hindu in practice recognises no society or community. This is the widest social group that the Hindus evolved and is therefore the limit of his allegiance, of his social relations, of his loyalties. It is the bed-rock on which the Hindu social organisation is built. Modern pseudo-sociologists of India have claimed many virtues for it and some Hindu and non-Hindu writers have seen in it the very essence of Hindu culture. They argue that the joint family suppresses the selfishness of individualism, by regulating rigidly the conduct of individuals in relation to a wider community; that it modifies the evils of private property, by vesting proprietorship in a larger whole; that it renders the essential social services such as old age pension, unemployment insurance, etc. to the importance of which Europe has only awakened recently and so on. It is unnecessary to go into these arguments. Every primitive institution is based on communal welfare. The whole theory of primitive tribalism is that and nothing more; but it cannot therefore be argued that it is better to live in a state of totemic tribalism than to evolve higher social organisations.

The joint family is nothing more than the survival of the primitive familial community which before the conception of society had dawned on man created round itself walls of blood relationship and economic identity. It subordinated the individual to the group (family), provided him with a code of morals, with duties and obligations and modified his "enlightened selfishness" by the ties of family. That it was a great step from primitive life to civilisation would easily be granted. It provided an organised life, by establishing a principle of social obedience. At all times, the central difficulty of civilisation has been the establishment of a principle of obedience, receiving universal acceptance as just and natural, and to which the people will subordinate their wills. In primitive and "savage" societies this was provided by the loyalty to the tribe which was enforced by *tabus* and *manas*. But it is essential to remember that the totemic tribe is a family *united together in blood relationship* with the totem. Thus the members, say of the Eagle tribe, are blood relations through the common fictitious eagle ancestor. As Longfellow says in *Hiawatha:*

> From what ancestral totem
> Be it eagle, bear or beaver
> They descended, this we know not.

No doubt such a relationship is purely imaginary but the important point is that the primitive mind could trace the principles of loyalty and voluntary obedience only through blood.

The change from the fictitious family to the real family as the unit is an important one in social growth. The patriarchal (or the matriarchal) family in which the paterfamilias is the undisputed master and exacts obedience from the rest is a known stage in the history of civilisation. But in most civilised societies it led to a further broadening of the social bases, mainly by two processes. First, by the limitation of the family, from the wide community of all blood relations that it originally was, to a strictly individualistic conception of it—as of father and children; secondly, by the gradual evolution of a conception of obligations and duties, transcending the family and extending to the whole community. In India, the system of the joint family not only persisted but grew in strength as a result of the absence of these two processes. Besides the non-existence of a unified central authority, be it of a king or of a church, to adjust legislation to social needs tended to crystallise customs and strengthen institutions which had the blessings of old law-givers. It should be remembered that the Hindu kings had no legislative authority. They did not promulgate codes, or modify laws. Nor have the Hindus had at any time a supreme religious authority —a sovereign pontiff or a church council entitled to change the Smritis. This we shall discuss later. Here it is sufficient to say that since neither church nor state existed with authority over Hindu social order, the institutions which had the authority of law-givers, or existed from ancient days could not be changed except by local or family practices (Dēsāchāra or Kulāchāra).

What has been the effect of this two-faced

institution, the caste and the joint family, on the Hindu peoples? Primarily, it has tended to sub-divide the social organism in such a way as to make the units smaller and smaller and unrelated to the general society. *Thus it denies the entire theory of community* and bases the organisation of Hindu life on the opposite principle of disintegration and division. From the point of view of the joint family and the sub-caste, the Hindus are no more than an inchoate mass of small units, not only unrelated to each other, but incapable of being related to each other as no marriage is permitted between them and social relations are rendered difficult as a result of interdictions on food. Secondly, the system enshrines and upholds the principle of inequality as each sub-caste considers itself superior to most if not to all other sub-castes.

Recently Indian leaders have begun to realise the evils of "Caste-ism". Now it will be seen that this caste-ism has nothing to do with *Chāturvarnya* or the four-fold division of caste. There is no common Sudra feeling, no appeal to Sudra unity, or even to Brahmin unity. Caste-ism is the loyalty to the sub-caste translated into politics. This is unavoidable as long as the conception of the sub-caste exists, for that is the one and permanent loyalty that the Hindu has inherited. In fact, no organisation of society on the basis of equality is possible so long as the sub-caste and the joint family exist.

Thirdly, this twin institution bases itself on, and in consequence emphasises at every turn, the principle of segregation and exclusiveness. The sub-caste would cease to exist if inter-marriage and inter-dining were extended beyond its frontiers. Naturally therefore, the whole power of the institution is turned against any attempt to break down the restrictions of food and marriage. No wonder that Tagore was moved to speak of Hindu social organisations as walls which shut out "the sunshine of thought and the breath of life", and an outside observer, to speak in terms of bitterness as follows:

"The high metaphysics of the Upanishads and the ethics of the Gita have been reduced to mere words by the tyranny of caste. Emphasising the unity of the whole world, animate and inanimate, India has yet fostered a social system which has divided her children into watertight compartments, divided them from one another, generation to generation for endless centuries. It has exposed her to foreign conquests which have left her poor and weak and worst of all she has become the home of untouchability and unapproachability which have branded her with the curse of Cain".*

There can be no denying that the organisation of Hindu life on the basis of the sub-caste or the joint family extinguishes the social sense, the feeling of obligation to a social whole and thereby renders the conception of a unified Hindu society impossible. It is neither the Hindu religion, nor even the four-fold division of caste but Hindu law that has branded India with the curse of Cain. As we saw religion has but little to do with the social institutions of the Hindus, and a man can remain a Hindu even if he repudiates its social institutions. Many sects of Hinduism actually so repudiate them and are still considered Hindu, which is clear enough evidence that these institutions are unrelated to religion. The idea of the four-fold division—the so-called four castes—is of integration, not of division.

* Prof. A. R. Wadia: *Contemporary Indian Philosophy*, p. 368.

It is the conception of a *single community* arranged in four layers and is therefore not in itself responsible for the anarchy of Hindu social life. The "sub-castes", except perhaps in the case of the Brahmins, have no organic connection with the main castes or varnas. It would therefore be wrong to blame *Chāturvarnya* for the evils of Hindu disintegration. The real fault lies with Hindu law which by its prohibition upholds the divisions and renders normal readjustments impossible.

Untouchability

One of the major facts of Hindu life is the existence of a system known as untouchability. The Indian Constitution has abolished untouchability and made its practice a penal offence. Legally therefore, untouchability is no longer a part of either Hindu or Indian life. Today the Harijans enjoy the same legal rights as the other castes. They attend the same schools and colleges and are given special facilities in the matter of education. They are not prevented from practising any profession they choose. They are recruited into every branch of public service, and Central and State Cabinets include members of these communities. Adult franchise has placed a weapon of great power in their hands, and the provision in the Constitution which reserves a certain number of seats for them in every legislature has enabled them to play a not inconsiderable role in public life. No impartial observer would deny that with the achievement of independence a very great change in the position of the Harijan community has come about.

While all this is true, and it is undeniable that legal disabilities have vanished, it would be absurd to hold that the social disabilities of the untouchables have ceased to exist with the proclamation of the abolition of untouchability. Social institutions, coming down for at least three thousand years and woven into the very fabric of Hindu life, could not all of a sudden cease to function. Though the legal disabilities have vanished the social facts remain, no doubt in a modified form, and could be changed only through years of effort. It is therefore necessary to examine the relationship of the system of untouchability to the structure of Hindu life.

Theoretically, that is according to the doctrine of *Chāturvarnya* or the four-fold division of society, the untouchables are outside the caste-system (Avarnas), and are called the fifth (Panchamas). They do not fall within the Hindu social order. They were communities outside the pale of Hindu social conceptions, but even a casual examination would show that they were essential to the normal functioning of Hindu life. The *tabus* and *manas* of Hindu life made it impossible for members of the four castes to follow certain professions. The menial service of the community, professions which were said to pollute or degrade, were not for the members of the four *varnas.* Consequently, a parallel society came into existence consisting of castes, outside the four *varnas,* who would fulfil these necessary functions. Every Hindu village postulated a group of houses outside the normal village area, where these humble folk on whom depended the sanitation and other menial work of the village, lived in the most miserable conditions. If streets had to be cleaned, if dead cattle had to be removed, if heavy agricultural labour had to be undertaken (in some areas) the members of the four castes had to depend on the fifth.

Their position, when the system functioned in its pristine glory, was in many ways worse than that of slavery. The slave at least was a chattel of the master and therefore he stood in an individual relation to his owner. Considerations of economic self-interest and even human feelings modified the barbarism of personal slavery. But even these mitigating factors did not apply to the system of untouchability, which was, it would be seen on examination, a system of *communal slave holding.* Instead of an individual owning slaves, each village held the untouchable families attached to it in a kind of communal slavery. No personal or social considerations were permitted in the least degree to modify the rigour of the system. No individual of the "higher" castes was supposed to have any personal relations with an untouchable.

But the strange thing was that the untouchables themselves lived within a caste organisation of their own. The system of joint family and sub-caste functioned among them also. Among them no less than among caste Hindus, there was an infinite gradation of sub-castes, each claiming superiority over the other. Untouchable society was in fact an imitation of Hindu life, in all its weaknesses, often enforcing among themselves social distinctions as rigid as among caste Hindus, and consequently as broken up and divided as the other.

It will thus be seen that while legal disabilities may vanish and untouchability in the sense of physical enforcement of pollution, refusal of facilities, etc., may be made penal and may indeed fall into desuetude as they have already done in many places, a parallel, subordinate and segregated society performing functions allotted by custom cannot be divorced from the structure of Hindu life. It continues as economic factor, and as a basis of Hindu village organisation.

Today a crisis faces the Hindu social system because though the parallel society of the so-called untouchables is still functioning in rural India, even there it has been undermined to its foundations. Under the combined onslaught of political changes, upheaval among the Harijans themselves, and it must be added, the social conscience of high-caste Hindus, both the theoretical basis of the parallel society, and its practical working have begun to give way. The political changes which give them the right to vote, reserved seats for them in the legislature, local institutions and, more important than all, in the village panchayats have made the Harijans conscious of their strength. Recruitment to the services and sharing of power at the highest levels have also been important factors. The community projects and national extension services have brought new ideas to the villages and introduced them to new ways of life. In the circumstances, the parallel society, segregated, confined to menial and degrading work, and kept out of the life of the village, can no longer function.

With the breakdown of the parallel society, the Hindu social structure that will survive will not be the same for which Manu legislated and to which caste-society has clung through centuries. The absorption of the Harijans and the tribal people into the general body of Hinduism will mean the disappearance of *Chāturvarnya* even as a conception. Hindu society such as we have known it at least from the time of the Buddha would then have undergone a transformation more radical than that which the Buddha attempted and more comprehensive than that which Sankara conceived.

Women in the Hindu Family

One of the major problems of Hindu social life is the position accorded to women in the Hindu joint family. Basically the Hindu social system proceeds on the assumption that the daughter never belonged to it. A girl born into a family is, according to old thinkers, like an ornament held in pawn to be surrendered to the rightful owner when he demands it. Yāska's *Nirukta* (11-4 Anandashrama Edition, p. 208) declares: "They give away to others the female children. There exist *dāna, vikraya* and *atisarga* of the female but not of the male." *Dāna,* means gift, *vikraya* means sale, and *atisarga* means abandonment. Durgacharya, the commentator explains these three methods of the disposal of daughters as giving away in marriage (*dāna*), as acceptance of payment for marriage (*vikraya)* and freedom to choose (*atisarga*). The persistence of the tradition of the female child being unwelcome in the Hindu family would show that Yāska's three methods of disposal of daughters were not merely theoretical but a description and rationalisation of the customs which the society of his time accepted which, without gloss, meant gift, sale or abandonment of the female child. In fact, the theory of the Hindu family does not contemplate daughters except as children. Every girl was presumed to marry and join some other family group as a wife where her rights though limited were defined. But as a daughter she had no rights in a Hindu family. This conception of the daughter being only held in trust for her legitimate owner posed no serious problem so long as there was child marriage and in fact compulsory marriage of all women in orthodox Hindu society. Today the problem is basically different. The raising of the age of marriage by legislation has created for the Hindu society the problem of the unmarried daughter. Besides as modern society does not provide such short cuts as infanticide and *atisarga* (abandonment) and there are no convents and nunneries in Hindu religion to which unwanted daughters can be dedicated—a form of *atisarga* highly approved by the religious—the issue has become one of urgency. The claim of the daughter to inherit her share in the family into which she is born—especially if she prefers to remain unmarried, is a denial of the very basis of the Hindu joint family. In any case, the unmarried woman introduces into the Hindu joint family an element altogether alien to Hindu conception and the recognition of her claims, which it is no longer possible to resist, will be a major breach in the citadel of Hindu social organisation.

The problem of the wife's property is equally complicated. If women are entitled to separate estates, either through inheritance, *Stridhan* or by acquisition, the indissoluble character of the Hindu marriage will disappear with it. It cannot be too strongly emphasised that the complete economic dependence of women is a necessary postulate of the indissoluble marriage in the patriarchal family. The acquisition of private property by women and their right to maintenance in case of separation involve nothing short of the formulation of a new code of marriage and family laws.

The claim of the widow to an independent share in the estate of her husband also changes the basic conception of the Hindu family. A financially independent widow permitted by law to remarry negates the conception of the permanence of family ties, the change of *gotra*, the acceptance of the new family and all other consequences of the sacramental marriage of the Hindus. A widow who does not remain a member of her late husband's family repudiates the conception of Hindu marriage.

It will be clear from the above discussion that the claim of the daughter, wife and widow to share in the property of the family involves a revolution, unseen but fundamental, in Hindu life. New conditions have created new problems. The unmarried daughter, the economically independent wife, the remarried widow, these are problems which the sociologists of ancient India did not have to deal with. The daughter was legislated out of existence: the wife became part of the husband's family and the widow was presumed to have died. These solutions were simple. Today however the position is different. Though Hindu law still refuses to face these issues squarely it is recognised that the problem has become urgent and any solution would involve a radical change in Hindu law.* The personal law of the Hindus, jealously safeguarded for so long by orthodoxy and maintained even under Muslim and Christian rule, has visibly broken down

* See the introduction. Legislation has changed all this.

in the face of economic claims of women.

Hindu orthodoxy undermined its own citadel when it permitted the education of women. It is true that neither Hindu religion nor Hindu tradition discouraged education among women. From the earliest days of Indian history we know of women who were thinkers, poets and scholars, but education was not widespread. Where it existed it was confined to the Brahmins and in exceptional cases to royal and noble families. But today the case is different. Women's education is evenly spread over all classes. If the Hindus desired to safeguard their worn-out institutions they should have kept their women in ignorance, emphasising to them as the immutable law, the doctrine of *pati-devata*, the husband-god. Though the orthodox did not fail to observe the disastrous results that would follow the education of women, and attempted in the beginning to deny it to their own children, they were unable to prevent the middle classes from educating their girls. The rise of new social classes in India based mainly on Western education put a premium on educated women even from the point of view of marriage. Naturally, educated women cannot be forced to believe in the ideal of *pati-devata* and to be content with the faith that the service and worship of the husband, however degraded, immoral and unmanly he be—is equal to worship of god himself. The ancient Hindu ideals of womanhood therefore came in for examination and criticism in the light of reason and common sense. The compulsory merging of the woman's individuality in that of the man, they came to see, had no justification in reason or in religion. Fortunately Hindu tradition is not only that of Nalayini, the meek devoted wife nursing her leprous husband and humiliating herself in every way, but equally that of Draupadi, faithful and devoted but dynamic and determined, following her husbands in their exile but always egging them on to action, rousing them in times of their dejection, and of Satyabhama accompanying her husband to battle-fields, Lopamudra and Arundhati as partners of their husbands in their mission—these are also in the orthodox tradition of Hinduism.

Also it is important to remember that Hindu religion has never taught the inferiority of women. There is no parallel in Hinduism to the story of man's Fall as a result of Eve's temptation and no stigma attached to womanhood as a whole. Ardhanareeswara, the god who is conceived half-woman and half-man, represents the integral view of Hindu religion in relation to woman, and this is emphasised by such popular notions as *Sita* Ram, *Radha* Krishna and *Gouri* Sankar. It is the law of the Hindus and not their religion which denies women property rights, used to compel girls to marry before puberty, and denied the right of re-marriage to widows. The last two have been changed by legislation and the first is being modified* without in the least affecting Hindu religion.

Further, education and intellectual discontent are inseparable. The awakening of thought in women has led to their increased participation in all fields of work. From the first days of the non-co-operation movement Gandhiji appealed directly to the women of India and his confidence in them was amply rewarded, for women were everywhere in the fore-front of the great struggle. In picketing liquor shops, in enforcing the boycott of foreign cloth, and in undertaking civil disobedience they shamed men in such a way that Gandhiji

* Since changed.

continuously spoke of them as the main support of his movement. From the social point of view the important thing was not the great role they played in the national struggle, but the defiance of social *tabus,* the breakdown of caste restrictions, the loosening of the social bondage in which they were held.

As equal participation of women in the struggle became the motto of the Satyagraha movement, the attitude of women underwent a profound change. Generation after generation of women growing up in an atmosphere not only of tension, but calling for every sacrifice involved the breakdown of traditional conceptions. When independence was achieved the position that women occupied in India's political and social life came as a surprise to the outside world accustomed to think of Hindu women, as being backward, uneducated and held down by a reactionary social order. It was significant of the great change that had come over India that as Governors, Cabinet Ministers and as Ambassadors, Indian women should have made their mark. But the significant thing in India is not the distinction achieved by a few women of genius but the change that has taken place in the villages, in the rural areas, among classes and castes, so far considered as orthodox or backward, where also women have been released in a very great measure from the social bondage that custom and conservatism had imposed on them.

The education of women and their political awakening have sharpened the axe with which to clear away the wild growths of Hindu social life. Education involves new moral and ethical conceptions and an unchanging moral code laid down two thousand years ago or based on the growth of local customs cannot satisfy an educated mind. It may be argued that the rigid code of the Catholic Church has not been weakened as a result of the education of women or their participation in political life and that similarly it does not necessarily follow that education should break down the social code of Hinduism. That argument is based on a fallacy. The social code of the Catholics so far as it is governed by the Church is not immutable. The Church through the Papacy provides a machinery of constant re-interpretation to suit the changing moral opinion of the world. The absence of social authority makes such gradual modification impossible in the case of the Hindus.

The re-examination of the principles of Hindu life by the women themselves is the greatest challenge that Hindu society faces today. That urge for re-examination comes primarily from the awakening of their minds to changed social needs; from a rising discontent with an utterly unsatisfying ideal, which taking refuge behind tradition, denies them the basic rights necessary for a free and independent life; from their ambition arising from education and from the heroic experience of two generations of national struggle to participate in the life of the nation and shape its future. The women's movement in India views Indian society as a whole and attacks it from the point of view of practical needs and immediate problems arising both from economic disabilities and social tensions. It is not the agitation of reformers, men moved by ideals to demand changes in social structure. The impetus in this case comes from the most conservative section of society—women—and it is they who provide the driving force behind the demand for social changes. Hindu social anarchy never faced such a challenge in the past.

The cumulative effect of women's awakening

and their claim to social equality may be described as nothing less than the reorganisation of Hindu society on a modern basis. The acceptance of the least important of their claims, for instance, the right of daughters to inheritance, would be a radical innovation affecting the basic conception of the Hindu family, while the gradual enforcement of the major items of their programme, rights to property, freedom of divorce and right of civil marriage would create a revolution in Hindu society establishing for it a modern code of laws, a new morality and a new principle of social relationships. The system of joint-family (the sub-caste) would disappear; the institutes of ancient law-givers would give place to rational codes; customs and practices which exist on the pretended sanction of religion, but which are merely the results of social reaction would be discarded. The modernisation of Hindu life and its re-invigoration may therefore legitimately be said to depend on the claims to social equality put forward by women. This is what the present legislation before parliament seeks to do; and when that legislation is passed a major revolution in Indian society would have taken place.

Custom as King

The fragmentation of social life which is the outstanding characteristic of Hindu organisation has had one result, the consequences of which it is impossible to exaggerate. It negatived the principle of social obedience except within the limited sphere of the joint family and the sub-caste and thereby prevented the growth of a feeling of social solidarity. The principle of authority on which national and social organisation is erected was, therefore, absent among the Hindus at all times in the past. Hindu life consequently developed as a wild and unregulated growth. Every kind of custom however poisonous, came to be tolerated and received sanction under the cover of religion. The practices of the Kāpālikas—including, it is said, the use of human flesh in worship—*sati,* marriage before puberty, dedication of women to the temples and other equally obnoxious customs which were at one time prevalent in different parts of India met with no social anathema. In fact, orthodox Hindu attitude to such practices—never widely prevalent and limited always to certain areas or communities—was that if people considered such practices as sanctioned by religion, it was not anyone's duty to interfere with them. The Kāpālika worship, and the more extravagant forms of the tantrism were considered by conservative opinion as being as orthodox as the performance of sandhya or daily prayer, or worship at a temple.

In the absence of state and religious authority, custom naturally usurped the functions of religion and arrogated to itself through pseudo-sacred writings the character of divine ordinances. Till the East India Company, through the agitation of Ram Mohan Roy, took up the question of *sati,* there was no instance of an exercise of state authority for the purpose of prohibiting anti-social customs. The case of *sati* is particularly interesting. It was not, as European critics fondly believe, a very widely prevalent practice. It was not practised anywhere in South India. In North India also it seems to have been confined to royal and noble families, and in their case also but rarely was the practice followed. And yet undoubtedly immolation on the pyre of the dead husband was considered a very meritorious act, and those who performed it were honoured as saints. The social conscience of the community never rose up against it. In prohibiting its practice and in making infanticide—again a custom prevalent only among certain communities—a crime, the East India Company took an unprecedented step. It attempted to regulate Hindu social life through state action. The experience of the great uprising of 1857-58, a contributing factor of which was the action of the Company's government affecting the social habits of the Hindus, acted as a warning and from that time, the Hindus were permitted to wallow in the mire of their own social customs. Non-intervention in social matters became the accepted policy of the British Government, though it was partially modified when the Montagu-Chelmsford reforms gave the people of India some voice in legislation.

The enthronement of social customs, widely different and often conflicting, as orthodox Hinduism, with religious sanction behind it, had been to a large extent facilitated originally by the establishment of Muslim authority in the Gangetic Valley. Though Hindu political thought never accepted the right of kings to legislate in social matters, the doctrine of the king being the regulator of the age (Rājā Kālasya Kāranam) laid on him the duty of preventing the growth of unorthodox custom. But with the arrival of Islam in India the new conception of a divinely revealed social order (and law) came to be widely accepted. The Islamic state has no legislative authority as its law is based on the divinely revealed Koran or on practices which have been authoritatively declared as flowing from such divine authority. The validity of new practices is dependent on the *fatwas* of religious doctors. In the parts of India which came under Muslim sway, Hindu social life was totally divorced from the state. The Muslim kings, following the practice of the Khalifs allowed the Hindus to be governed by their own customs and by their caste *panchayats*. As the Muslim conception of kingly duty did not involve social legislation, they could do nothing but allow custom to have unrestricted sway in communal matters. Thus, though Akbar was violently opposed to the practice of *sati* and himself intervened to save more than one unfortunate woman, the moghul state could not prohibit this inhuman practice. In the result, Muslim rule in North India had the extraordinary effect of encouraging an anarchic growth of social customs, each claiming to be orthodox and each asserting its sacred character.

It would, however, be wrong to conclude that the co-existence of a religion like Islam with such clear-cut principles and with a uniform social theory, based on equality led only to the growth of reaction and the crystallisation of custom among the Hindus. The influence of Islam on the thinking mind of India was profound, but here, as at a later time, it led, in the absence of general authority, to the formation of new sects. Upsurges of opinion which could have led to a national reorganisation of Hindu society frittered away into sects and groups. Individual religious leaders like Kabir and Nanak protested against the growth of irreligious customs and practices. Their influence was great in their lifetime and if a national authority was in existence, it would have been forced to give legislative effect to the demands for radical reforms. But the movements that they started to reform Hindu society, as many great men from the time of Buddha had done before them, resulted only in the formation of new sects and the fabric of Hindu society remained unaffected.

There is another aspect of Hindu-Muslim contact, as affecting Hindu society, to which attention may be drawn here. The Hindu states which remained independent like Vijayanagar or the Rajput Kingdoms, or which came to be organised on the basis of a Hindu revival, like the Maratha Empire, became the champions of Hinduism on its defensive. The *raison d'etre* of their existence was as a sanctuary and refuge of orthodoxy. A society on the defensive is necessarily more reactionary, more anxious to preserve than to reform, to be apologists for what had been inherited, good, bad or indifferent. These states therefore considered it to be their true function to conserve the *dharma* and uphold the customs and practices of the past. The duty of kings to regulate customs and to weed out what was injurious to the body social was obscured by the more urgent duty of warding off attacks from the enemies of the *dharma*. Thus, both in the areas under direct Muslim rule, and in the kingdoms of the Hindus, social thought became defensive and every kind of custom came to be considered as sacred and inviolable.

Another result of Muslim invasions was the

effect on Hindu law itself. Till the establishment of Islamic authority Hindu law had continued in an imperceptible manner to grow and develop. The great commentators had interpreted the *Smritis* with an understanding of social forces. But with the Muslim invasion new and unprecedented problems faced the Hindu legists. Their primary function became to save the Hindu society from the great threat that Islam presented. From the 13th century, the Nibandha literature (*smriti* digests) becomes overweighted with its *prayaschitta* section. The emphasis is on social rigidity and on punishments in case of deviation. The literature of the Nibandhas during this period is voluminous, but there is not one—including the legal encyclopaedia written under the orders of Todar Mal in the time of Akbar—which breathes a spirit of liberal interpretation as in the case of Medhathidhi. The commentators of the Smritis had become the champions of social reaction. It is under this blighting shadow that Hindu society continued to live till recently though in many of its aspects, outside the sphere of social custom, it has been modified by British legislation in India.

Limits of Toleration

The principle of toleration is one of the tests of civilised life: and yet no one can deny that it has certain limitations. Law is one expression of that limitation; social conscience is another. No one would argue that toleration should extend to cannibalism or to witchcraft, though in certain stages of human evolution both were considered normal. Nor would it be argued that on the ground of toleration, the right of slave-holding should be upheld though till quite recently the institution of slavery was not considered abnormal. These and other similar practices of the past are prohibited by law. But apart from what law refuses to tolerate, in civilised no less than in ordered primitive societies, there are customs and practices which the social conscience of the community does not tolerate. To give one instance, in many countries, there is no law against nudity but the community would not tolerate such a practice in the open. In Hindu society alone no limit seems ever to have been set on the principle of toleration. Nude men can walk about freely in the streets of India and will even be permitted to ride on elephants amidst wide acclamation in the streets, on the pretext of religious sanctity. In fact, this abuse of tolerance is one of the reasons for the elevation of fantastic practices to the position of religious customs. It is the fundamental faith of every Hindu that salvation could be attained by genuine faith in any *marga* (path). Does not Krishna himself say that "He gives reward to each according to his form of worship"? Therefore, though one may prefer one's own path as being superior, the validity of another man's belief cannot be questioned. This is indeed a noble doctrine, a principle of broad catholicism in which the Hindus take genuine pride, and yet, it is this principle of the validity of every belief genuinely held which leads Hindus to tolerate the most absurd creeds as recognised sects of Hinduism. Creeds which elevate obscene ceremonies to the position of mystic sacraments, practices based on the belief that virtue resides in certain trees and plants are tolerated with an indifference to social sense. The fact is that the Hindus have never defined the limits of toleration. It is no justification to argue that toleration of beliefs is merely a recognition of human fallibility and therefore any interference with it may lead to the suppression of truth. It is not suggested that there should be any limitation of belief. It may be my belief that ritual murder alone will give the results I desire. No doubt I am entitled to that belief but the translation of that belief into practice is another matter. The question involved in that case is not one of religious toleration but of social defence. In fact, on examination it will be seen that the whole organisation of social life is based on a definition of the limits of toleration. A toleration which is unlimited is licence and anarchy and no society could be organised on that basis. It is this abuse of the principle of toleration, a refusal to define its limits—reinforced by the absence of any machinery for the enforcement—that has led to the social anarchy of Hinduism.

Legislation and Society

We have seen that the social institutions of the Hindu people are the results of certain historical factors and that they are in no way concerned with religion. They are upheld by secular law and not by religious sanction. The caste organisation, the joint family, the rights of inheritance, and the complex of social relations arising from all these are legal and not religious. They are man-made institutions upheld by man-made law.

The great legal codes of Hinduism have no general application today, for except in relation to personal law, they have been replaced by other codes. But even in regard to personal law it is not what Manu and other ancient law-givers laid down that is now authoritative; it is what the great commentators have expounded as law that applies in different parts of the country. This is clear enough proof that Hindu society was legislating for itself in a crude and primitive way. There is indeed reason to think that even when the Manava Dharma Sastra came to be codified many portions were already out of date and unenforceable. Oliver Wendel Holmes has very wisely observed that the legislation of today is to meet the social needs of yesterday, that law as a conservative force must necessarily lag behind social necessities.

The great Hindu codes, which embodied the legal thought and practice of many centuries preceding their codification, were no doubt progressive enough in their day, that is, they were not very far removed from the social conscience of the people. Also, their evolution shows that there was no immutability attached to them. The commentaries modified many of the injunctions of the codes or through interpretation made them more in accordance with the social conscience of the time. Thus the great weakness of Hindu social life is not that the laws on which it is based have not undergone change but that the changes have been sporadic, local and dependent on the ingenuity of individual commentators. They were not in any sense a continuous renovation of legal principles and a conscious attempt to adjust laws to changing social needs. Besides, their influence was generally local. Thus the Mayukha interpretation which gives greater property rights to women is confined to Bombay and Dayabaga is confined to Bengal. In fact, there are local variations practically in every part of India in regard to vital matters like marriage, adoption, etc. Local customs repudiate clear provisions of law even in orthodox Brahmin communities. For instance, it is a basic doctrine of Hindu marriage that sapindas cannot be united in matrimony, all *Smritis* being unanimous on this point. And yet in South India, marriage to one's sister's daughter is a recognised custom among certain classes of Brahmins. In the matter of adoption again, though the law enunciates one set of principles, the practice in different parts and in different communities varies greatly.

The reason for this lack of direction of social ideals preventing the growth of unauthorised customs and anti-social usages was undoubtedly the absence of political unity in India. India as a whole was never under a single political authority and the matter for surprise therefore is not that there is so much variation, but that there should be even this extent of uniformity giving to Hindu law the general characteristics of a single code. The codified

Smritis were able to maintain their authority, no doubt subject to local modifications, without the advantage of a single political authority over the entire country to give them sanction of support. That is no doubt a political miracle evidencing the basic unity of the Hindu people.

The absence of a national authority with plenary powers to legislate for the vast majority of Hindus has now been remedied. For the first time in history, there is now in India an authority created by the people themselves, which has not only affirmed its right to legislate for the Hindus but is able to exact obedience. The Constitution of India, as we shall see later, both through the Fundamental Rights which are declared therein and through the Directive Principles incorporated into it, not only has assumed but has proclaimed in the clearest terms its right and duty to legislate for social needs. It has abolished untouchability and declared its practice a penal offence. It has by law established equality of opportunity for men and women. From the beginning the Indian Parliament has been active in the matter of social legislation, whether it be called the Hindu code or by another name.

What the legislature is unconsciously seeking to do is to convert the unorganised masses of Hindus into a single community. Vaguely, reformers during the last 25 years had felt the need of welding the Hindus together into a people. The credit for making this idea popular, though in an aggressive way, must go to Swami Shraddhanand who initiated the *sanghatan* movement in 1925. *Sanghatan* means integration, and what Shraddhanand, a great leader of the Arya Samaj, set out to do was to create at least in the Punjab, a Hindu society as united and as closely knit together as the Muslims. But the very idea of community involves common ideals and common interests. The caste and the joint family clearly negate any such ideas, and no *sanghatan* is possible so long as these institutions control Hindu life. The Sikhs, the Arya Samajists and the Radhaswamis alone of all the divisions of Hinduism have a sense of community. They have consciously cultivated the ideal of a single community and that has been their strength. The Arya Samaj is controlled through central institutions and accepts the principle of authority and is able to enforce obedience. The Radhaswami sect has a pontiff. But Hinduism as a whole, containing as it does, a vast variety of sects can have no such religious authority. Its reorganisation must, therefore, come through the secular state, and only through the activity of the state could Hindu *sanghatan* be achieved.

That reorganisation actually began in a small way with the legislatures which the Montagu-Chelmsford reforms brought into existence. The legislative machinery of dyarchy* was only partially representative of Indian opinion but it was the first that had ever been established in India which had authority to legislate for the vast majority of Hindu population. And yet it passed some very important pieces of legislation; the Sarda Act raising the age of consent for marriage to fourteen in the case of girls, the Civil Marriage Act, validating marriage between Hindus of different castes, and the Earnings of Learning Act. Each one of these three Acts touched the basic conceptions of Hindu society. We saw how child marriage was closely connected

* A system of divided government introduced by British Parliament in India in 1921.

with the Hindu doctrine of joint family which postulated the non-existence of unmarried daughters. The raising of the age of consent directly affected this, as the number of unmarried daughters in joint families created the problem of their inheritance. The Civil Marriage Act, legalising marriages between Hindus of different castes struck at the root of Hindu orthodoxy. The one nightmare of ancient Hindu law-givers was *varna sankara* —or the mixture of castes. All their anathemas are directed against this deadly sin. Of course, the marriage of Brahmins with women of other castes, being *anuloma* was permitted; but the reverse, the marriage of others with Brahmin women was something which it was too dreadful even to contemplate. *Varna sankara,* this is the *pratiloma* mixture of castes was in orthodox Hindu view, the end of all social order and the "immutable" law prohibiting *varna sankara* ceased to operate through the length and breadth of India by the Civil Marriage Act, though being permissive its immediate effect was limited. The Earnings of Learning Act also cut at the root of the joint family system. The basis of the joint family is the equal right of all members to the earnings of all. The earnings of members of the learned profession were by this Act excluded from the operations of the joint property rule. The legislature even under a foreign government was forced by the pressure of popular opinion to act in matters so fundamental to the traditional Hindu social order. The legislating state had come into existence.

That independent India's Parliament elected on adult franchise would not tolerate the social anarchy of Hinduism was clear from the beginning. The Constitution itself renders such an attitude of neutrality impossible as the Directive Principles incorporated in it go against some of the main features of Hindu social life. It is a legal and constitutional modification of the Hindu society, far-reaching in its consequences and revolutionary in its comprehensiveness, that the Indian Parliament is now seeking to accomplish by its social legislation.

Extent of Legislative Competence

The question therefore arises, how far a social revolution of this character can be accomplished through legislative processes. History, both ancient and modern, bears witness to the limits of legislative competence when it comes to inherited social traditions. From the time of Akhen-aton to Mustapha Kemal the history of nations tells the tragic tale of the failure of great revolutions undertaken through legislation. Akhen-aton's is the earliest record we have of a great king attempting to change the basis of a national society through decrees. It failed miserably, and almost brought the empire to ruin. Chin Shih Huan-ti, the first Chin Emperor of China, an equally determined innovator, decided to break with the past and even ordered all previous books and inscriptions to be destroyed so that the generations to come may not even know what the earlier traditions were. But the traditions were stronger, and even the books which he had destroyed with an astonishing thoroughness were either reproduced from memory or forged by the next generation. The French Revolution installed the Goddess of Reason and proceeded to reorder society on the basis of the rights of man and yet a few years later, an Emperor was crowned at Notre Dame with all the solemnity of

Catholic ceremony in the presence of the Pope himself. Mustapha Kemal was perhaps the most thorough social innovator through legislation. Fifteen years of Kemalist government altered the face of Turkey. The revealed code of the Koran and the *shariat* were replaced by new legislation, subject to continuous modification by Parliament. Family life was placed on a new footing by the abolition of polygamy, by the compulsory discarding of the veil, by the admission of women to all professions. Arabic script was replaced by the Roman, the flowing robes of the Ottoman gave place to Western dress. A revolution of an unprecedented character was planned and put through by parliamentary legislation. The attempt to pull out the roots of national life was made on an even larger scale in the Soviet Union, where the whole structure of society was changed by revolutionary legislation.

Leaving aside the question of the Soviet experiment, where the changes were brought about by revolution and upheld by a trained and disciplined body—the Communist Party—it has been a general criticism that social revolution through legislative action has at best yielded only partial results; that the overwhelming force of racial memories, tradition and the imperceptible influences of institutions have always asserted themselves at the end, silently modifying the nature of the change itself. It is pointed out that in India democracy itself—which is the very negation of caste—has assumed a new shape and form through the influence of caste; that as with some of the reforms in Turkey, the legal abolition of untouchability has not put an end to a notorious social fact.

While it is undoubtedly true that there are recognised limits to legislative competence, and reforms introduced by law are often transformed by the weight of social traditions, it is equally true that legislation alters the course of social evolution and even where it fails, modifies the structure rendering it impossible to restore the past in its entirety when reaction takes charge. Much of the legislation of the French Revolution continued even during the Bourbon restoration and an unbridgeable gulf existed between the *ancien régime* and the society that emerged in 19th century France. It was impossible for Louis XVIII, Charles and the White Terror to restore the society which met its doom in 1789.

Equally, the Kemalist Revolution, even if it has failed to Europeanise the Turks to the extent that Ataturk had hoped, has so modified the social structure that a return to a purely Islamic type of social order is no longer possible. If the effect of social tradition is permanent, so is the effect of a change once introduced in a society.

The true limits of legislative competence are to be found in the social conscience of the people. If legislation outruns the social urge, then it must remain largely ineffective, though in time it may help to create a social climate. If, on the other hand, the institutions of a people have become meaningless forms through the social urge of a people and the law and customs which uphold the institutions have been circumvented through legal fictions, then changes through legislation are no more than the formal ratification of changes which are already in operation. Prof. Dicey has demonstrated in his masterly analysis of the influence of public opinion on the law of modern England, how in recent times, the most important pieces of social legislation were enacted in Parliament only after the ideals they represented had achieved decisive victory in the country. In such cases legislation lags behind the advance in social conscience and cannot, in truth, be considered as more than legislative ratification of changes already accepted by the people.

There is a third area of legislation which is important in modern society; that is where legislation anticipates social needs. The process of continuous examination of social trends and the renovation of traditional institutions and social forms which every modern society accepts as necessary, leads inevitably to legislative enactments. Labour laws, social insurance, and care of children are but a few instances of this kind of activity. It is in this sphere that the modern state, whatever its character, is continuously active, thereby attempting to shape and modify society as a continuing process.

The legislation that the Hindu society has to undertake is not of the first kind, that is where revolutionary changes are sought to be imposed from the top. What is urgently required is the legislative ratification of social ideas already accepted, giving them universal application and a uniform character. As we have already emphasised, Hindu social conscience has been crying for basic changes in social structure for some time. The abolition of untouchability, for example, has been not only a major demand of our political parties, but one of the spheres of devoted activity by reformers of all castes during the last half a century. The demand for legislative action to give property rights to women and to secure modification in marriage laws has been widespread. The disruption of the joint family has already proceeded apace and legislation is now necessary only to control the legal effects of this breakdown. So, the legislative programme for the reorganisation of Hinduism is only in spheres where social conscience has been far in advance of laws and institutions.

The programme of legislation in the third sphere is not specifically related to Hindu institutions; but its effects on Hindu social life would be of a far-reaching character. To give but one illustration, the control of religious endowments by government or by bodies elected by legislature, cannot fail to have far-reaching social consequences. The free entry of all Hindus to public temples, a reform which was the result of sustained public agitation, undermines the religious sanctions of untouchability. Even measures like the abolition of Zamindari and the break-up of the large estates have profound social consequences. The poorer Brahmins who fulfil the priestly role in Hinduism have at all times been maintained by the landed gentry. There is no paid priesthood in Hinduism, but it was always considered a primary duty of the land-owning classes to feed and maintain the Brahmins. The disappearance of the landowner as a major element in Indian society would undoubtedly affect the position of the large body of poor Brahmins, on whom the rituals and ceremonials of society depend.

The modern state is based on the conception of a purposive organisation of society. It is not merely an administrative institution. Essentially, it represents the total life of the nation and exists in order to mould, direct and organise the complex of social forces according to the needs of the times. It controls all economic life and in many cases directly engages itself in economic operations. It seeks to control population, to distribute human material, to organise work, and through sanitation laws, public health arrangements and in a hundred other ways interferes with our daily habits. All these, when carefully examined, will be seen to have profound effects on our social behaviour and ultimately on the structure of society itself. What cannot be done by direct legislation, as being likely to arouse opposition, gets normally accepted when enforced piecemeal through municipal laws and other local regulations. More than all this, in States, which have lagged behind in political power and whose social institutions still bear a medieval imprint, the legislative activity of the state to bring society to the level attained in progressive countries will be continuous. Especially in India, as the last twelve years have clearly demonstrated, the state will concern itself more and more with the organisation of life in social and economic fields. That will be the real *sanghatan* of Hindu society.

That in this welding together, much that we now consider the differentiating characteristics of Hindu society will disappear is certain. In the past, the world had equated Hindu society with caste, untouchability, sacramental marriage, enforced widowhood and such other customs. When these have disappeared what would remain to identify the Hindus as a race? Surely the Hindu religion and the *samskaras* associated with it, a purified and invigorated social order based on the religion —these will still differentiate the Hindus from others. Whether much remains or only a little, it is clear that a legislating state and social anarchy cannot co-exist. The Constitution of India itself postulates the right of the people to change the conditions under which they live and as the bewildering confusion of Hindu life was the outcome of the absence of state-conception and political authority, the very creation of the state and the constitution with which it has clothed itself constitute a major challenge to Hindu society.

The Impacts

The Indian Constitution contains a declaration of Fundamental Rights and incorporates certain Directive Principles, which though not enforceable through courts, proclaim with emphasis the ideals for which the state stands. Some of the Fundamental Rights so enunciated and many of the principles laid down are in direct opposition to the Hindu conception of society. Also the constitution contains an open declaration that the State shall strive to promote the welfare of the people by securing and protecting as effectively as it may, a social order in which justice, social, economic and political shall prevail. This by itself is a denial of a social order based on *Chāturvarnya*. It states the opposition to the Hindu social ideas with absolute clarity. This is further emphasised by other directives which preach equality of opportunity, necessity for a uniform civil code, etc. The Constitution also embodies the gains of the social changes of the earlier period.

It fact, it may well be claimed that the Constitution is a solemn promise to the people of India that the legislature will do everything possible to renovate and rebuild society on new principles. Its impact, therefore, is specially important and deserves careful examination.

The most striking feature of the Indian Constitution is undoubtedly its acceptance of the fullest implication of democracy by basing it on adult franchise. Considering the fact that over 40 million persons are officially described as Scheduled Castes, which were previously subject to social disabilities based on untouchability, it will be clear that adult franchise has social implications far beyond its political significance. The Scheduled Castes are spread all over India; they form, in fact, the submerged base of Hindu society. To invest them with so large a share of political power means not merely an affirmation of their equality, but the placing of machinery in their hands with which to enforce their rights. Adult franchise has had other results. Many social groups, previously unaware of their strength and barely touched by the political changes that had taken place, suddenly realised that they were in a position to wield power.

The Padiyachis, previously a socially backward caste of whom but few people had heard, suddenly emerged after the elections of 1952-53 as a most powerful group in the Madras Legislature. They put forward social pretensions, called themselves *vahnikulam kshatriyas*—kshatriyas of the family of Fire, and took advantage of their numerical strength to demand a share in political power. In effect, they have brought about a revolution of no small significance in the Tamil area. Everywhere in India this process could be seen in varying degree. Traditionally powerful communities have had to yield place to others who have realised their strength in a political system based on adult franchise.

Another important result flowing from the Constitution has been the breakdown of the feudal traditions in the former Princely States. About a half of the territory of the present Indian Union was previously ruled by Indian Princes. The social integration in these States was based on the castes or groups to which the Ruling Family belonged. The Rajputs in Rajasthan shared power with the Rulers, and the other communities, even when they were rich and powerful, counted for little in the States.

In the Maratha states power belonged to the members of that community. In Travancore-Cochin power was mainly in the hands of the Nayars and other communities associated with the Rulers. The disappearance of Princely Rulers changed all this practically overnight. In the Rajasthan Cabinet for a time there was not a single Rajput. Their lands and *thikanas* have been taken away from them. They have, in fact, ceased to be a ruling community. A similar change has come over all the vast areas which once were ruled by Princes. Its social significance can well be imagined, especially when it is considered that most of the States in North India were citadels of orthodoxy to the very end.

The Impact of Communism

The effect of the Constitution and of the political forces it set in motion is continuous and almost imperceptible. It looks natural and logical and does not, therefore, arouse violent opposition. The same cannot be said of the challenge to Hindu society which Communism spells. Communism sets out primarily to reorganise society on a completely new basis, not merely to change its economy and its political forms, but transform society as a whole and build it up on new principles. The Communist doctrine postulates a classless society, based on the power of the proletariat. It clashes with every conception of Hindu life, caste, joint family, restrictions on marriage, food *tabus,* etc. In fact, there is no aspect of Hindu life which is not challenged by Communism. Every Communist has to accept and to practise in his own personal and party life, principles which contradict at every turn the accepted values of Hindu social life. This is one of the attractions of Communism to young and radical minds, which see that no other system repudiates so uncompromisingly the social principles against which they are in revolt. Gandhism, Socialism, Nationalism and all other political philosophies compromise with the practices of Hinduism and become "reformist" in their outlook, hoping to modify Hindu social institutions, partially by legislative action and partially through the operation of other forces—social and economic. Communism alone is uncompromising on this issue being based on a total denial of the validity of all Hindu social institutions. They recognise no caste, no joint family. Even their marriages are outside the social framework of the Hindus. The fact that the leaders of Communism in India are men and women belonging to high castes gives to this revolutionary approach to social problems an appeal which otherwise it might have lacked.

Not only in the direct work of the party, but in all their subsidiary activities, the Communists emphasise the challenge to Hindu social institutions. Their theatre, a most effective vehicle of propaganda, has this as its primary theme: the collapse of the walls of our social Jericho to the bugle call of the Communist Archangel. Their literature both "progressive" and Communist has the same object. In fact, their attack on the Hindu social system is meant to destroy it utterly, so as to create a social vacuum in which they could operate freely.

Even if we do not accept the Marxian view that social forms are determined by economic factors, no one can deny that economic stages mark new departures in social life. Hunters and fishermen transact their affairs on different lines from pastoral nomads. A rural community builds up its social life on principles which are different from those which operate in commercial societies. Paul Vinagradoff has analysed the difference in legal conceptions in societies organised on different principles of economic life. With the advance of civilisation, these customs are rationalised and become laws claiming authority, either from the state or the church, thereby also creating a machinery capable of changing the laws according to economic needs. With the Communist state, law becomes an instrument not for change but for the demolition of the social organisations of capitalist society. Basing themselves on the doctrine that social forms in a capitalist society have been determined by capitalism in its interests, the Communists attack them root and branch by denying their values and by holding up as the ideal a society built up entirely according to the principles of Marxism.

It would be nothing short of complacency to think that as Hindu institutions have withstood the challenge of Buddhism, Islam and Christianity, each of which in its turn denied the basic conceptions of Hindu society or challenged them on the religious and social plane, we have nothing to fear from the Communist assault. The circumstances are totally different. Islam and Christianity as rival organisations were unable to challenge Hinduism seriously because those who were converted to those religions had to leave the fold of Hinduism. Their attack was consequently from outside, and Hindu society had no difficulty in defending itself. By becoming Muslims or Christians, the Hindu converts were rendered unable to attack Hindu society from inside or to lead movements for reform. The Communists realised this weakness and even when they denounce every aspect of Hindu social life and deny in practice all the customs which unite the Hindus, they continue to live within the Hindu society. Their open defiance of caste rules, marriage customs, food *tabus,* etc. while remaining formally within Hinduism is the kind of menace that Hinduism is unable to deal with, as it has no machinery to enforce conformity.

The Impact of Industrial Society

The impact of industrial society is also a factor of considerable importance in transforming the social structure of the Hindus.

Caste system is to a very large extent related to village industries and handicrafts. A rural economy is the basis of both the joint family and of occupational castes. An industrial society cuts at the root of both. It is a noticeable fact that in large industrial areas, the Hindu social structure has already undergone radical changes. So far, the effect of these changes on the community in general was limited by the fact that industrialisation was confined to certain limited areas. But the developments of the last few years, especially community projects and national extension services, have been carrying into the rural areas the new ideas of the city. In fact, these schemes which already cover a considerable section of India's rural community, may be described as an attempt to urbanise our villages.

The political transformation of the villages through Gaon Sabhas—village councils—is already an accomplished fact. This has had remarkable effects in releasing new social forces and of upsetting the inherited structure of the villages. Today, in village councils the untouchable sits side by side with the Brahmin and the landowner. In many places members of the classes which were formerly socially depressed have been elected presidents. The important point is not so much the sharing of power in the villages by these classes, but the *abolition of the parallel society,* which is the traditional characteristic of Hindu rural life. With the disappearance of the parallel society and the twin settlements of caste and out-caste, the rural life of Hindus undergoes a change in a sphere where it had been entrenched for thousands of years. Hindu social orthodoxy has always been village-based. Neither the Muslims nor the British were able at any time to penetrate into that area. It is here, in this reserved area, that it is now being attacked.

The decay of handicrafts and hereditary occupations, which is inevitable in a society moving towards industrialisation, affects the social structure in a number of ways. Every Indian village had its blacksmiths, carpenters, potters, oilmen, weavers, leather workers and other recognised occupational castes. Though these may survive here and there, their economic position has been so undermined that they cannot continue any longer as organised castes. The potters' ware, for example, is now brought to the villagers' door-step from factories. With large-scale government subsidy the weavers may be able to survive, but the textile mills have taken over the duty of supplying the masses. The disappearance of occupational castes can no longer be prevented.

The extention of electric power to the villages and the distribution of major industries over wider areas, all over India, affect Hindu social life in many ways: electric power brings with it minor industries and helps to urbanise the village. When the first step from the house to the factory is taken, it also spells the doom of caste in that area. Small village factories kill caste even more effectively than common schools. The planned dispersal of industry, which takes every area of India into consideration is, therefore, a threat to Hindu ways of life.

The organisation of trade unions, an essential concomitant of industrialisation, operates as a major dissolvent of our stratified society. The vast majority of workers belong to the lower castes. The organisation of the mass of people into unions gives them political and industrial power and they gradually become affected by radical ideas. The awakening of labour in India is therefore also an awakening of the socially depressed classes to their rights as human beings.

The explosive character of modern technique, machinery, transport, living equipment, etc. is also not sufficiently recognised in India. The social implications of modern technology are very widespread. Caste and food restrictions cannot be enforced in railways; in fact, pollution by touch, which was strictly enforced in Kerala before the first war, broke down automatically as a result of railway travel. Hospitals where everyone is admitted equally, schools and colleges and other public institutions also helped to eliminate distinctions.

The Impact of Science

The impact of science on Hindu society has also been far-reaching. Strangely enough, of all major religions in the world, Hinduism has been the least affected by the advance of science. Many observant Europeans have noticed how the basic doctrines of Hindu religion fit in with the most advanced concepts of modern science. The great scientific controversies which shook Christian dogma to its foundations, like the Copernican system and the theory of evolution, do not seem to touch Hinduism, which in its higher spheres contradicts no scientific belief. But this cannot be said of many Hindu practices and some of their major social institutions. It is a well-known fact that of all nations today, the Hindus alone attach social value to astrology and attach importance to astronomical phenomena. Astrology may, in fact, be considered one of the basic factors of Hindu life. In normal and even highly-educated families no marriage can take place except on an auspicious day fixed by the position of stars. No marriage takes place unless horoscopes have been compared. Every ceremonial connected with a marriage is dependent on auspicious muhūrts fixed by astrologers. Many, among even the educated, do not set out for journeys without looking at the position of stars. In the orthodox Hindu State of Nepal, public functions depend on the position of stars. The great Hindu festival of Kumbh Mela depends on a combination of stars. Solar and lunar eclipses are days of sacredness because of some ancient beliefs. It is difficult for an outsider to understand to what extent astrology enters into the normal life of Hindus.

Naturally, the impact of science on this kind of belief is great. The educated man who consults the astrologer about an auspicious date for the marriage of his daughter is well aware that the position of the stars can have no influence on conjugal felicity. The political personages who dipped in the Ganga at Prayag on the day of Kumbh Mela could not have believed that special sacredness was attached to ablutions in the Ganga waters on that particular day. Science has demolished faith in such practices and what is now gone through is mainly a formality. The practice of vegetarianism—which is in no way connected with Hindu religion, but is followed by the higher castes as a part of religious custom—ceases to have meaning where it is scientifically proved that vegetable kingdom also possesses life and is subject to pain and pleasure in the same way as animals. Thus the impact of science on Hindu customs and practices has been of a far-reaching character and will be more so when scientific knowledge penetrates the masses:

The Impact of Thought

More important than science, for the knowledge of science must at all times be confined to a few, is Thought itself. The impact of thought has the most devastating force on social institutions. The man who questions a practice, or defies a custom, as a result of his own thinking, creates forces which in certain circumstances can be revolutionary. Especially in societies bound down by custom, thought and expression are potent dissolvents and legislation comes in to give form and sanction to thoughts which have already gained wide acceptance. In Hindu society thought had not abdicated its function. It was continuously examining the bases of Hindu social structure but owing to the reasons which we have analysed earlier, it only led to the creation of new sects, or new reformed groups. In the absence of a legislating state, there was no machinery for incorporating any new thought in the general body of Hindu tradition. Political disunity, which led to the existence of many jurisdictions, also prevented a general acceptance of reform all over India with the result that reformed groups were confined to the localities of origin. The difficulty of communications and the absence of a common language for cultural exchange in the 17th and 18th centuries when even the study of Sanskrit as the all-India vehicle of thought had fallen into decay made a nation-wide movement of thought well-nigh impossible. It was only by the middle of the third quarter of the 19th century that the situation began to change. A common vehicle for thought—the English language—became available to educated Indians to propagate their thought through the length and breadth of the country.

Also, from the beginning of the century, thought itself had taken a revolutionary turn. In the earlier period, even when the basis of Hindu social order was questioned, the forms of orthodoxy were generally maintained and the attempt always was to claim that the new thought was only an interpretation or a restoration of the true meaning. But Ram Mohan Roy and Keshab Chandra Sen made no such claim. Their attacks on the Hindu society were not on the basis of authority but of reason. Though Swami Dayanand Saraswati in his *Satyartha Prakash* follows the traditional method of claiming that he was revealing the true meaning of the Vedas, there is no doubt that his teaching, which repudiated most of the Hindu social traditions, was even more revolutionary than the reasoned liberalism of Ram Mohan Roy and the Bengal Reformers.

Even the thought of the orthodox had become dynamic. Swami Vivekananda—the champion of Vedanta and the reviver of Hindu orthodoxy—was a radical thinker who did not hesitate to denounce Hindu social institutions. It is he who proclaimed before an astonished world that caste had nothing to do with Hinduism. "Beginning from Buddha to Ram Mohan Roy," said he, "every one made the mistake of holding caste to be a religious institution. . . . But in spite of all the ravings of the priests, caste is simply a crystallised social institution, which after doing its service is now filling the atmosphere of India with stink." This is indeed Thought in its most revolutionary form. Since Vivekananda's time caste has had no defenders. The problem that remained was solely that of clearing the debris and building on the foundations. But that was not possible so long as India was not free. The legislature of "British" India even if it were minded to legislate on social matters had jurisdiction over only three-fifths of Indian territory. Over the other two-fifths there ruled hereditary Indian Princes who, with one outstanding exception, were ranged on the side of the dead past. The exception was Sayaji Rao Gaekwad, a true social revolutionary, who foresaw the problems of Hindu society and endeavoured to deal with them comprehensively in his small state. But as against one Sayaji Rao Gaekwad, there were over 130 others, many of whom enforced untouchability in their territories. In many States of Rajasthan the untouchables were not allowed to go to the same schools till the day of independence. These States in many cases permitted child marriage, punished as a criminal offender any wife who left her husband's roof, etc. In States like Travancore, Cochin and Mysore, social reform had made considerable advance, but generally speaking, the Princely States had remained reserved areas for social obscurantism till their disappearance in 1949.

The Constitution recognises the fact that legislation to reform Hindu society is one of the primary duties of the Indian Parliament.

Article 25 of the Indian Constitution reads as follows:

> " 25 (1) Subject to public order, morality and health and to other provisions of this Part, all persons are equally entitled to freedom of conscience, and the right freely to profess, practise and propagate religion;
>
> (2) Nothing in his article shall...prevent the State from making any law
>
> (a) regulating or restricting any economic, financial, political and other secular activity which may be associated with religious practice;
>
> (b) *providing for social welfare and reform* or throwing open of Hindu religious institutions of a public character to all classes and sections of Hindus."

It will be noted that legislation providing for social welfare and reform is specially saved, thereby serving notice on orthodoxy that freedom of religion does not include the right of protection to customs, usages and practices which the social conscience of the people has rejected. Another important aspect of this provision is that, for the first time, the limits of toleration are defined. As we noticed before, the great weakness of Hinduism was that it set no limit to the doctrine of tolerance in religious beliefs and practices. That inherent and grave defect has been remedied by this clause.

The impact of other religions and societies on Hinduism need not be discussed here. To a large extent they have helped to produce the changed climate of thought in India. The co-existence of Christian and Islamic societies outside the closed social order of Hinduism produced changes, not so much in social life, as in the realm of thought, leading in the first instance to movements which crystallised into new sects. It was only when it began to act as a leaven and thereby produce a revolution in thought among the Hindus themselves, that the conflict between ideas and institutions began to manifest itself.

The Prospects

The transformation of the inchoate mass of Hindu peoples into a community has been a slow process, but clearly it is taking place now. In place of the elementary conceptions of the joint family and sub-caste, we are now working our way towards a single community held together not merely by a common culture, but by common social institutions. A genuine Hindu feeling has come into existence today which manifests itself occasionally in very crude forms. It may be conceded that this is not altogether a new phenomenon in the history of the Hindus. That such a feeling existed in the third and fourth centuries of the Christian era is clear from the fact that there was an organised effort to re-write the *puranas* and to create a body of literature with a new Hindu ideology. Again, a genuine Hindu feeling is noticeable at the time of the Muslim conquest of North India and threat to the people of the South. But that feeling in the face of danger was defensive and not reformatory. It was an effort to close the ranks and hold together in the face of a grave crisis. As Mr. Ketkar has pointed out in his *History of Caste,* the overthrow of Hindu rule in the Gangetic Valley led to a great increase in the prestige of the Brahmins. The secular "Kshatriya" power was broken, and the consequent leadership of the Brahmins led to an extreme religious reaction. Caste became more rigid and social customs, without the directing hand of the secular State, usurped the authority of religion. While Hindu feeling gained strength, it failed to evolve a valid conception of a Hindu community as a result of the disintegrating influence of caste.

It must, however, be conceded that the vigorous reaction of the Brahmins at the time saved Hindu society from dissolution. While the classes which had assumed the functions of the Kshatriyas compromised with Islam for the sake of political power—thereby yielding their social leadership—the Brahmins protected what they considered to be the *Dharma* to the best of their ability. Under their influence Hinduism withdrew more and more into its shell and its anti-social characteristics became exaggerated. But it is well to remember that but for Brahmin leadership at the time there would perhaps have been no Hinduism left today for others to reform or to regenerate.

The service which a small priestly class rendered to a whole people at the time of the destruction of their political power is paralleled only by the action of the Jewish rabbis when the Temple was destroyed and Jews dispersed by the Romans. At the time when the Jewish people sank into despair, a group of learned men under Johanan ben Zakkai established the great academy at Jabneh in the heart of Roman Palestine itself and guarded zealously the doctrine of Judaism. It sent its messages to the Jewish people dispersed all over the world and thus saved Judaism for the future. That is what the Brahmins did in the 13th and the 14th centuries in the Gangetic Valley.

While such an attitude of rigid exclusiveness was necessary for the safety of Hinduism, it did not help the cause of progress. A religion on the defensive has to be reactionary and consequently, the growth of Hindu feeling at that time did not create conditions suitable for a re-organisation of a Hindu social life.

Today the situation is different. The Hindu feeling which has developed is primarily secular and not religious. It is not the outcome of any threat to Hinduism, for the Hindu religion has emerged triumphant from its 800 years of confrontation with Islam, and the less dangerous but more subtle attack of Christianity. Today there is no danger to Hinduism and the urge for a re-organisation of society proceeds from other causes, as we have already noticed. Its religious basis, if it can be said to have a conscious religious basis, is to make the religious truths of Hinduism shine without being obscured by outworn customs and irrational social forms.

Secondly, the social upsurge today is not a matter either for the intellectuals or for a great Reformer. It is not a case of a new Buddha rising or a movement among certain classes, like the one which resulted in the Brahmo Samaj. It is an uprising of the lower classes, and the underprivileged sections. The transfer of political power has provided the masses with dynamite for the destruction of social institutions based on privilege or on hereditary inequality. The forward impulse that the rise of these groups to power has given is a new factor of the widest significance.

Again, the integration of the country and the facilities of modern technical civilisation provide a qualitative difference to the conditions that prevailed in the time of the Buddha, Sankara, Kabir and Ram Mohan Roy. In their times distances rendered all-India repercussion to ideas impossible. Reforms and changes tended, therefore, to be local and to create further divisions in an already divided society. With the development of railways, airlines, posts and telegraphs, distance has been practically annihilated. The range of Buddha's activities was confined to Magadha; that of Gandhiji extended to every nook and corner of India. Sankara had to go walking from place to place and then could only reach the *élite*. Today, the message of change is published through thousands of papers, through the radio and the cinema. The cinema especially, through its indirect approach, touches every aspect of social life, the family, matrimonial conditions, caste, social relationships, etc. in a way which changes opinion in these matters more effectively than the most persuasive reasoning is able to do. As we have seen, the vast concentration of people in centres of industry has already created social problems which the Hindus had never contemplated. The silent operation of these forces in the circumstances of daily life is fast creating a revolution which neither caste nor custom can arrest or limit.

Movements like the *Bhoodan Yajna* initiated by Vinoba Bhave are attempts to tackle these problems from the point of view of an awakened social conscience. The importance of rousing the community to a recognition of the injustices in which we are living and of creating a climate of opinion in favour of radical change are obvious and what Shri Vinoba and his associates are doing is therefore of primary significance. But a solution of the problem cannot come from them. It can only come through conscious and purposive action by the State.

Organised popular political activity postulates the principle that society is subject to human ordering. This is the vital difference between democracy and all other forms of government. Autocracy does not attempt to change the social order as it is based on no conscious social urge, but on the convictions or the whims of a ruler. But a State based on the activity of the people consciously tries to order society according to its ideas.

These factors and above all the desire of the Hindus to take their place with the progressive nations of the world, which is one of the major motivating forces in India today, gives to the movement for social revolution an urgency which it never had before. The Hindus today realise, perhaps vaguely, that their integration into a community, with purposive direction of social forces and energies and fulfilling the ethical and moral conceptions of their best minds is the first duty of the Indian State. They realise that for centuries now, Hindu society has been in the grip of a wasting disease because the energies of the whole body could not be concentrated on any common purpose. It is now realised that to resist the ravages of this disease in our body-social the application of palliatives would no longer be sufficient. The body itself should be made stronger, healthier and more vigorous and the rejuvenation, if it is to be successful, must enable us to conserve our strength. The weakening of thought, the absence of enterprise and initiative and the general decline of vigour—factors which dragged the Hindus down during the last few hundred years—will finally disappear only when society becomes organised to receive ideas, which are its food, and to transform those ideas into practice.

Religion and Society

If the joint family, caste and the variety of customs which now constitute the social structure of Hinduism, are destroyed or replaced what, it may be asked, will be left which is characteristically Hindu? The worship of the plethora of divinities is already dead among all but the uneducated. If the social structure is also destroyed, then it may be feared there will be no Hinduism, except perhaps a quantum of vague philosophical theories based on the Absolute, *Advaita* with its twin corollaries of *Maya* and *Karma*. To many intellectual Hindus, this is all that Hinduism means even today. Shri C. Rajagopalachari, one of the most distinguished Indians of our generation, in his book *Hinduism, Doctrine and Way of Life*, presents the creed of a vedantin as nothing beyond this. If this is all that Hinduism is, clearly it cannot be a religion for the people for it remains a matter of individual faith according to the development of each man, and provides him with no spiritual sustenance beyond the dream of liberation, through *Jnana* or spiritual knowledge attained through self-discipline and work. No one would deny that the doctrines which Shri Rajagopalachari has explained with lucidity constitute an essential aspect of Hinduism. But it is not the totality of Hindu teaching. Even the Gita provides for *Bhakti* or devotion and the teachings of all religious sects, while accepting the fundamental conception of *Vedanta,* transcend its coldly rational conclusions. If *Vedanta* were all that would be left after a rational reorganisation of Hindu society, then in my view it would be far better to leave that society as it is, with its innumerable shortcomings but with a living faith, with its rich and glowing mythology embodying many fundamental truths, with its symbols and rituals which deeply affect the emotions of a whole people than to leave it attenuated with only a philosophical background and a doctrine of liberation. But fortunately, as Shri Rajagopalachari has himself explained in many other books, Hinduism is much more than a philosophy or a number of philosophical schools. It is a religion giving sustenance to every aspect of human life, and the modification of laws or the abolition of customs will no more adversely affect the religion of Hinduism than the discarding of old and dirty clothes and wearing of clean and new ones affect a man.

The social institutions of Hinduism are in no way integrally connected with either the outer or the inner forms of religion. The inner forms of religion, its ethic, its general philosophy, its doctrines of direct realisation, through *karma, jnana* and *bhakti,* these are in no way connected with the customs, social forms and personal laws prevalent among the Hindus. No one would argue that if the joint family were to be abolished by law today, or caste ceased to operate as an institution, Hindu religious thought would be affected. The question however is not merely about the doctrines of the Hindu religion, but the outer aspects of Hinduism, its forms of public worship, its festivals, its rituals and its control over conduct, i.e. its practical ethics. These are as important for a religion as a complete set of unexceptionable doctrines. It may be argued that a change in marriage laws will affect the bonds of family, which after all, are the final bonds of society, that the breakdown of caste, may at least for a time lead to social disharmonies.

As these views are fairly widely held, they require to be examined carefully.

Family is a social conception not a religious one. In the Hindu system itself different kinds of families operate, both the patriarchal and matriarchal systems, systems based on sacramental marriage and others based on custom. Hindu law is said to prohibit divorce, but there are large communities all over India professing Hinduism as a religion which permit divorce, and even by custom sanction remarriage of widows. Their Hinduism is not affected in any way. As we have pointed out there are Brahmin communities of unexceptionable orthodoxy who marry their own sisters' children—something utterly obnoxious to the Hindu law-givers' conception of marriage. Indeed there is no particular social institution which is so universally accepted among the Hindus to enable us to say that it is a part of Hinduism.

So far as the outward forms of religion are concerned, the worship in temples, the great festivals, the outward symbols of sects and groups, the mutts, monasteries and ashrams, the practice of sanyas and all other things which differentiate Hinduism from other religions will continue unaffected by any social reform or modernisation of laws that might be enforced. Whatever philosophers and intellectuals may believe or preach, it is this aspect of Hinduism which makes it a religion, instead of a philosophy. It is the neglect of this aspect, the life of the Hindu people in their religion, and an emphasis on philosophy to the exclusion of outer forms that will destroy the soul of Hinduism. Comte was but the last of a long line of philosophers who believed that an effective ethic can be evolved solely on the basis of philosophy—a fallacy to which Shri Rajagopalachari also seems to become an unsuspecting prey. In his brilliant exposition of Hinduism he equates Vedanta with Hinduism and preaches it as an ultimate ethic.* But the greatest thinkers of Vedanta, Sankara and Ramanuja, had a different view. Sankara, the champion of Advaita, was also the reformer of the ritual of Saktism, who taught the new worship of Devi, known as *Samayachara,* who composed innumerable hymns of ecstatic beauty. He realised clearly that both worship,

* While this criticism is strictly correct in respect of *Hinduism, Doctrine and Way of Life,* Shri Rajagopalachari has in many other works emphasised the emotional and *Bhakti* aspects of Hindu religion.

including contemplation, ritual and other aspects of spiritual discipline, suitable for all levels of minds, and a doctrine based on reason, were equally important for a religion. So far as Ramanuja was concerned, the lesson was even more clearly emphasised. As Prof. K. V. Rangaswamy Aiyangar states: "To the comprehensive philosophy which vindicated the rights and obligations of the free soul, Ramanuja attached a religious side which gave wide scope for spiritual emotion."

It would be clear that any re-examination of social values and reform of secular institutions by normal legislative processes would not affect Hindu religion. Whatever the nature of our society, both the inner and outer forms of our religion will continue to mould our ethic and our life, for religious beliefs will operate through society, however constituted.

The relation between religion and society, in short, is not based on particular institutions, however ancient, because institutions must of necessity reflect the ideas of a particular period. It is when institutions, through which alone social forces can work, do not provide for the three principles of self-preservation, continued examination and reconstruction, that decadence sets in, and true religion gets separated from social forms. For reasons which we have analysed earlier, the Hindu social institutions, especially Hindu law and custom, did not during the last 1,500 years provide for such a continuous readjustment. The effect of this on our social growth has been disastrous. The effects on Hindu religion have been equally disastrous, because anachronistic social institutions have obscured the resplendent light of its religious truths. The contradictions between our religious principles and our social practices became so glaring that many critics, including Indian thinkers of undoubted eminence, felt that Hindu religion itself was responsible for the evils of Hindu social life.

For a proper appreciation of Hinduism, with its basic principles of equality, of purposive action for *loka samgraha* (social good) unattached to personal interests, of the perfectability of man, it is necessary that the present social order of the Hindu people should not be mixed up with it. Once the difference is understood, the present apparent contradictions would not affect our faith or lend themselves to a misunderstanding of our religious doctrines.

It will thus be seen that a reorganisation of Hindu social life is necessary from the point of view of religion itself. Broadly speaking, religion can work only through social institutions, and it has been the misfortune of Hinduism that the institutions through which it had to work, and with which it came to be identified, represented not the living social conscience of the people, but the dead urges of a remote past. Hindu orthodoxy which fights social reform in the mistaken belief that it is defending Hinduism and opposing something which aims to undermine Sanatana Dharma is, therefore, doing its own cause the gravest possible harm.

Conclusion

The thesis of this book, as explained at the outset, is to demonstrate that the Hindu people, if they are to regain their position as an effective branch of the human race, must transform themselves into a single social organism, governed by laws which approximate to their ethical conception; further that the new institutions must be of a character which would permit them constantly to renovate themselves by adjustments to suit changing needs; in short, the Hindus should transform themselves from an unorganised mass of ill-defined social groups into a single community. This is possible only if we accept the ideal of an unceasing activity directed towards the development of the physical, moral and intellectual life of the people as a whole. The theory of Hindu social life does not accept the idea of a community, for it is based on division not on unity. But during the last few `decades new ideas have entered Hindu life, and the idea of community has taken root as a result both of opposition to other integrated communities like Islam and Christianity and of the penetration of Western thought. A new and perhaps equally important cause which contributed to the growth of Hindu consciousness was the political organisation of the Hindu masses, and their participation in the fight for independence. Few people realised that political independence based on democracy involved the breakdown of orthodoxy itself. Mass political activity—as exemplified by the Congress under Gandhiji's leadership——involved two basic postulates, both dangerous to orthodoxy and in combination utterly destructive of its foundations. The first was that the Indian people (of whom the vast majority and the unshakable base are Hindus) constitute a single political community, though the Congress as a secular and non-communal organisation, thought of India as a plural society. Whether a single Indian community, or a plural society, it meant of necessity the importation into Hindu social life of the new doctrine of integration not based even on *Chāturvarnya* but on a single Hindu people.

Secondly, as we have emphasised already, mass political activity meant the acceptance of the democratic ideal for independent India, and that meant inescapably the acceptance of the view that society is subject to human ordering. Democracy claims an omnipotence which kings and emperors could never imagine, especially in the social field. Democracy has a social content which is not obvious at first sight but is inherent in it. It depends for its strength on the masses, and the masses once awakened to social purposes insist on emancipation. This is all the more so in the case of a country like India where a mass national movement for over quarter of a century activated the lower classes for gaining political strength. Social emancipation had of necessity to find an important place in the national programme, if the mass movements were to gain strength and become politically effective. The urge for a unified Hindu people is, therefore, an inheritance of our national movement.

Two other factors may be alluded to as having contributed to the growth of new social urges. The system of education which the British introduced in India was secular and therefore based on a denial of inspired authority. The social thought which gained prevalence among the educated classes came from

John Stuart Mill and Herbert Spencer and other rationalist thinkers, in whose scheme of things religion and dogma had no place, Anglo-Indian education was also given to all who could pay for it, without reference to caste or status in society. Thus there was born among the educated classes a widespread denial of the social values of Hindu institutions.

Further, the advantage that orthodoxy had in the fact that India had no history and that therefore ancient authority could be claimed for quite modern customs, slowly vanished as the researches of scholars reconstructed the political evolution and social growth of Hinduism. The canons of modern criticism began to be applied to the texts which had for so long a time been held up as sacrosanct. It was for example found that *Manava Dharma Sastra* or the code of Manu was after all not so old as the orthodox liked to claim and further that many of the *Smritis* were later fabrications. The fact that the caste system was not in operation in Vedic times came as a shock to those who had proclaimed it to be divinely ordained. Equally, practices like child marriage which orthodoxy claimed to be based on religion were found on examination not to have been prevalent in the period of the epics.

Reconstruction of history has been equally destructive to the sanctity of many widely prevalent customs. The patient researches of historians have helped to demonstrate that when the Hindus were a vigorous and dynamic race, many of the social aberrations which are now claimed to be based on religion had no validity at all. Thus, for example, it was the belief till recent times that Hindu religion prohibited the crossing of the seas. The Brahmins enforced *prayaschittas* on all who dared to break this custom and even liberal politicians are known to have gone to Canossa and purged themselves of their sin of journeying across to other continents. The Maharajas of Cochin and Travancore, until a few years ago, prohibited entry into temples to people who had visited Europe. Historical research knocked the bottom out of this belief. The history of Hindu empires in Java, Sumatra, Siam, Camboj, etc. and the records of many scholars who had visited China by the sea route have clearly established that in the days of political independence no restrictions existed on travel by sea.

Again, in the case of a custom like widow re-marriage which till recently was held to be contrary to Hindu religion we have incontestable historical evidence that Chandragupta II married the widow of his brother. Even in the Ramayana there is clear evidence of the prevalence of the custom of *levirate*, as may be seen from the arguments which Sita uses to persuade Lakshmana to go in search of Rama who had been enticed away by the golden deer.

Even the doctrine of a golden age, the favourite myth of the orthodox, has helped to popularise the theory of social change. A golden age in the past necessarily postulates a present degeneracy: a fall from the ideal conditions of the past. The conceptions of an unchanging social order and of a golden age are, therefore, contradictory and irreconcilable. Degeneration involves a theory of social regression and invites an examination of the validity of the laws and customs in force.

These and other factors have contributed to the new social urge which has imperceptibly changed the character of Hindu society. It was Auguste Comte who emphasised the inseparable connection of the physical, intellectual and moral aspects of life, with material conditions. The cumulative effect of the changed material conditions and the intellectual awakening has been to expose the contradiction between the growing sense of community and the existing social order of division. In fact, in India social conscience has outstripped social practice. This is incontrovertibly attested by the fact that in all the movements meant to ameliorate the miseries arising from social evils it is the higher caste Hindus that have toiled and sacrificed most.

When social feeling has reached that stage of awakening, when wide resentment is caused by the effects of outmoded customs, or when society in general, while paying lip service to them, circumvents their operations then the field is clear for effective general legislation. It is the argument of this book that the translation of the idea of the community from the realm of the mind to the realm of activity through the modification of laws has now been rendered possible both by the awakening of the Hindu mind and by the existence of an effective machinery of legislation entitled to general obedience and capable of enforcing it. The argument that legislation by itself can do but little to reform societies is perhaps true: but the important difference is this. Where social conscience has already come to believe in the necessity of change, legislation can give to such changes, direction, form and, what is more, continuity.

It is also true that the experience of societies changed all at once by law is not sufficient to warrant a faith in revolution by legislation. When the state's structure enforcing legislation has endured and the social revolution inaugurated by it does not in its turn become static, but is subjected to continuous re-examination, even revolutionary social orders have remained fairly stable. In fact, it can hardly be denied that continuous legislative activity consolidating the social development of the people has been one of the determining factors of history. Hindu law itself was no more than the consolidation of the social feeling of the time when it was codified and it is that law, with the modifications introduced at different times by commentators that has shaped Hindu life. The complaint is not that Hindu law did not undergo changes, but that the changes have been sporadic, local, and not based on any comprehensive social thinking. The legislation that can remodel Hindu society should aim not merely at correcting evils or changing customs that have become obsolete, as in the past, but at the consolidation of the progress of the Hindu mind in terms of law; that is the translation of the social urges of the present time into institutions.

Suitable and timely modification of institutions is the primary function of the state. Every society provides for itself the machinery to modify and renovate its structure. Even the most rigidly conservative of human organisations, the Roman Catholic Church, has at all times had a machinery for incorporating the changes necessitated by time. The Ecumenical Councils, the Curia and the Pontificate itself provide machinery for such constant modifications. This, in fact, is the differentiating characteristic of a progressive society. In Hinduism, unfortunately this machinery did not exist till now.

The realisation has now dawned upon the Hindus that unless the sanction of law is behind social changes, every effort in the direction of reform will only lead to further chaos. In fact, the social anarchy in Hinduism is as much due to unregulated reform in the past which tended to be local and sectional as to the disintegrating forces of the divisive caste.

The challenge that Hindu society faces today is something which it never had to face in history. It is the authority of a national state armed with plenary legislative powers and motivated by a desire to bring Hindu institutions in step with new ideas. Once this movement starts, it cannot stop. There may be periods of greater or lesser activity, but the change has to be continuous as social values will change and will clamour for enforcement through legislation. A legislating state and a static society cannot exist side by side. Besides the tremendous economic revolution which is taking place in India, the consequences of which no one can foresee, will generate new social forces which will be reflected in the social legislation of the future, and in the ordering of our new society. That this renovation of the social energies would only lead to a better ordered life should be obvious. It should be equally clear that it would help to re-establish Hinduism in its position of honour among the religions of the world.